The Breakup 2.0

The Breakup 2.0

Disconnecting over New Media

Ilana Gershon

Cornell University Press

Ithaca and London

First published 2010 by Cornell University Press

Printed in the United States of America

Library of Congress Cataloging-in-Publication Data

Gershon, Ilana.
    The breakup 2.0 : disconnecting over new media / Ilana Gershon.
      p. cm.
    Includes bibliographical references and index.
    ISBN 978-0-8014-4859-1 (cloth : alk. paper)
  1. Digital media—Social aspects. 2. Digital media—Psychological aspects. 3. Separation (Psychology)—Technological innovations—Social aspects. 4. Rejection (Psychology)—Technological innovations—Social aspects. 5. Interpersonal communication—Technological innovations—Social aspects. 6. Online etiquette. I. Title.
    HM851.G4723   2010
    303.48'33—dc22   2010001008

For my students

Contents

Acknowledgments

My biggest debt is to my students, who provided me with this research topic and then generously and patiently tolerated my enthusiasm for teaching almost every theoretical point by using examples about how people use technologies to break up. My undergraduates responded by explaining to me how their practices were changing, and corrected my misapprehensions. My graduate students in my seminar on publics were invaluable in helping me work out the ideas for the last chapter.

While my students introduced me to this project, Lauren Leve told me this should be a book. I can't remember exactly what we were talking about—probably neoliberalism—when I mentioned to her that I had an interesting conversation in class about mediated breakups. I told her I was thinking of writing an article or two about new media and breakups, but I hadn't decided yet whether I should. Lauren told me that it had to be a book. And, of course, she was right.

I want to thank everyone who shared their stories and thoughts with me about how they and others have been using communicative technologies in the often painful process of disconnecting with others. I have promised to use pseudonyms or else I would thank them here by name. Several people helped me to either find or process interviews and sources: Stephen Berrey, Aditi Deo, Flory Gingging, Melissa Hunt, Nancy Lightfoot, Meredith Morris, Ted Striphas, Matt Van Hoose, and Rosalyn Wells.

I have enjoyed the intellectual friendship of wonderful colleagues and friends who helped me work out precisely what I wanted to say and suggested directions I could take: Elizabeth Armstrong, Richard Bauman, Karen Bowdre, Don Brenneis, Max Dawson, Melissa Demian, Susan Gal, Lisa Gitelman, Jane Goodman, Mary Gray, David Hakken, Joan Hawkins, Barbara Klinger, Jean Lave, David Lipset, Ray McDermott, Joel Robbins, Jennifer Robinson, Susan Seizer, Michael Silverstein, Teri Silvio, Bonnie Urciuoli, Hervé Varenne, Heidi Voskuhl, and Bjoern Weiler. I am particularly grateful to Mary Gray and Max Dawson for their suggestions on how to think about the "newness" of new media. And my thanks to Joshua Malitsky for being patient as I interrupted our writing to conduct interviews filled with loud laughter next door.

I had kind readers who warned me when my sentences were too convoluted and reminded me when I needed to explain more. I am so grateful to the following for all their thoughtful interventions: Allison Alexy, Litz Brown, Amy Cohen, Kon Dierks, Lynn Fisher, Susan Lepselter, Lauren Morris MacLean, Joshua Malitsky, and Teri Silvio.

My two editors, Fran Benson and Peter Wissoker, were enthusiastic and encouraging, giving me invaluable advice throughout this process. And my two anonymous reviewers helped tremendously to make this a much better book.

I also want to thank my mother for supporting me throughout with good humor.

My biggest thanks to the person who was forced to read sentences over and over again, and to be part of countless conversations about mediated breakups: David Fisher.

Introduction

I had the idea for a book on how the medium shapes the breakup message while I was teaching an undergraduate class on language and culture. Early in the semester I ask my students to write down individually all the rules they know for a first date. I use this exercise to help them realize that they are part of a community with shared and often unspoken expectations. This question unfailingly reveals that they share assumptions about proper behavior with their classmates, people they often have never spoken to before. My students all seem to agree on certain basics. People should dress well, but not too well because one should not seem to be trying too hard. The date should involve a nice restaurant or a movie. Many seem to assume that the people on this date are straight. My students even have predictable disagreements about who pays, although no one suggests at first that the woman should pay. I ask this question every year, and I have started to get bored with the answers.

Three years ago, I looked at my lecture notes and thought, "Oh no, I am supposed to ask that question again." On a whim, I asked instead: "What counts as a bad breakup?" I was expecting answers like, "I found my girlfriend in bed with someone else," or "We yelled at each other until three in the morning," or "He never returned my favorite DVDs." Instead, my students all told me about *mediated breakups*—that is, breakups by texting (sending a text message), or by Facebook (a popular social networking Web site).[1] One man admitted he sent his best friend to tell his girlfriend, knowing as he spoke that he was confessing to breaking up poorly. Every woman in the class whirled around to stare at him in horror. His protest that his ex-girlfriend was psycho did not seem to help his case—it was clear to me that he had just lost any chance of turning my class into a dating opportunity. On hearing that the mark of a bad breakup was a mediated message of some form, I began to suspect I had a new research project.

One of the reasons I was so interested in this question was that, from one perspective, it doesn't matter what medium you use to break up. If you are ending a relationship, what does it matter if the ending is announced on cream stationery, by text message, or in a face-to-face conversation? Breaking up is breaking up. Yet for everyone I have spoken to about this, it matters: When someone says "she broke up with me by texting," not much more needs to

1. Facebook is a collection of profiles that people post as self-description, with the common assumption that each profile indexes a single person, with chosen events in their life recorded on their profile through photos or text. Not all the photos or texts on a profile will be posted by the person who manages that profile. Others in the person's network can add to the profile by sending Facebook gifts, writing publicly available text on a person's wall (i.e., wall posts), or adding photographs with the person tagged (i.e., marking the photo with the person's name so it can be found quickly). A person with the profile's password can refuse to include a self-description, detag or untag photos, and delete wall posts or gifts. Looking at a profile on Facebook is to look at a collection of information about a person compiled by a social network, but selected by the profile's password-holder(s). These profiles are understood by the people I interviewed to be intrinsically linked to one's offline life. While there may be profiles that have no obvious living offline anchor, students understand these Facebook "fake profiles" to be exceptions.

be said. So much about the breakup seems to have been summed up in that one sentence. Breaking up face-to-face is widely considered the ideal way to end a relationship.[2] Most people told me that breaking up through the wrong medium can signal to others the initiator's cowardice, lack of respect, callousness, or indifference. People's ideas about the medium shape the ways that medium will deliver a message. No matter what is actually said, the medium becomes part of what is being communicated. Sometimes the medium is in synch with the message, and sometimes it is so out of synch with the message that the message is undercut. To say: "I have so much work and other stuff going on in my life right now, I can't be with anyone" as the away message on an instant messaging[3] profile is using too public and informal a medium for the message to be taken as a serious and respectful gesture. When you are breaking up, the medium is part of the message.

The medium shapes the message in part because people have *media ideologies* that shape the ways they think about and use different media. Media ideologies are a set of beliefs about communicative technologies with which users and designers explain perceived media structure and meaning.[4] That is to say, what people think about the media they use will shape the way they use media. I discuss media ideologies and the other key concepts I mention in this introduction—remediation and idioms of practice—in much more depth in the first three chapters.

In my interviews with college students, they often talked to me about how formal e-mail is as a medium. They would compare

---

2. Only 4 people out of 472 people I surveyed or interviewed felt otherwise.

3. Instant messaging (IM) refers to communications between people in real time over the Internet using text.

4. For a parallel definition of *language ideologies,* see Silverstein 1979, 193.

e-mail to a letter, mentioning how they both require a salutation and a closing. E-mail, they insisted, was a medium for expressing important information or for professional correspondence. They often use e-mail to communicate with professors, bosses, parents, and grandparents, but rarely with friends. E-mail's formality for college students is part of their media ideology about e-mail; it affects how they use e-mail and the explanations they give for how e-mail as a medium affects the meaning of what is said by e-mail.

Yet not everyone shares the same media ideology about e-mail as my students. I certainly don't. I was surprised to find out that for my students, e-mail was a formal medium. I am not alone in this. Every professor I mentioned this to was surprised to find out college students think of e-mail as formal. For me, e-mail is informal—I can write short notes to someone, and it often feels like it takes less time than a phone call. I also don't need to find a stamp and a mailbox. I see e-mail on a continuum between formal and informal; the more I choose to make the e-mail look like a standard letter, the more formal it becomes. But, for me, it lacks some of the formality and care of a letter. Both my students and I are using e-mail, and we use it often to communicate with each other. Yet different aspects of e-mail are important to us as we develop media ideologies about what e-mail is as a medium and what it can accomplish. For my students, e-mail's ability to resemble a letter marks it as more formal. For me, it is the many ways in which e-mail can be written more quickly and more haphazardly than a letter that helps make it an informal medium. This is one of the ways that people experience new communicative technologies as new—they don't necessarily share the same media ideologies with people they communicate with regularly.

Notice that in talking about different people's media ideologies about e-mail, it quickly becomes necessary to discuss people's media ideologies about letters as well. Because college students think of letters as formal, e-mail's resemblance to letters (in their minds) makes e-mail, by analogy, formal as well. Media ideologies about one medium are always affected by the media ideologies people have about other media. How you think about texting is linked to how you think about calling someone on your cell phone, which is linked to how you think about instant messaging and so on. Sometimes what is important about a medium is how much it resembles another medium—like e-mail and letters for college students. Sometimes what is important is how distinct the medium is from other media—like e-mail and letters for me. Jay David Bolter and Richard Grusin use the term "remediation" to describe the ways that people interlink media, suggesting that people define every technology in terms of the other communicative technologies available to them (1999, 28). In terms of breaking up, this means that when someone breaks up by e-mail, it matters that they could also have chosen to break up by phone, voice mail, instant messaging, or letter. People are aware of the options and have distinct ideas about these options. Ideas about what one can do in one medium are always implicitly understood in terms of what one can do in every other medium available. These tacit comparisons shape how people will interpret the medium used to break up.

Media ideologies aren't based only on how a medium is defined in contrast with other media. Media ideologies also revolve around people's ideas about how the structure of technology shapes the ways you can use it to communicate. When I was talking to college students about texting breakup, some focused on the 160-character limit of a text message, and felt that people simply couldn't provide adequate and necessary explanations in such a short message. Others discussed how you could get this message anywhere—at home, at a bar, or in a meeting—as one criterion for why it was a poor choice for this type of message. Not all aspects of how a technology is structured are equally important to people, and people's media ideologies and practices will determine what aspect of the technology becomes significant in a given context. While most students agreed that texting wasn't the ideal way to break up with someone, the reasons they gave differed because of how they understood and used the technology in other situations.

People don't concoct their media ideologies on their own; they develop their beliefs about media and ways of using media within *idioms of practice*. By idioms of practice, I mean that people figure out together how to use different media and often agree on the appropriate social uses of technology by asking advice and sharing stories with each other. They end up using these technologies with the distinctive and communal flair that has been attributed to dialects, or idioms. Idioms of practice point to how people have implicit and explicit intuitions about using different technologies that they have developed with their friends, family members, and coworkers. For example, after breaking up, the two people have to figure out how to let their friends know that they are no longer together. Is it appropriate to let people know by Facebook immediately, or should people wait to tell their close friends by phone or in person? Different groups of friends decide together what is the most appropriate medium to spread the news of a breakup. Idioms of practice emerge out of collective discussions and shared practices. Often the implicit intuitions don't become apparent until someone violates an expectation—perhaps by breaking up using the wrong medium.

Part of the reason why communicative technologies encourage people to form idioms of practice is that these technologies, particularly new technologies, present people with a range of problems, both social and technical. People come up with solutions to these problems through conversations with people they know. For example, when trying to figure out how to argue with their lovers by text message, students will ask their friends what they should text next. Arguing by text message is a social skill that people have to develop—they discuss with friends the timing of when to send the angry text message, or how to capture what they want to say in the texting format. As people try to figure out the morally or socially appropriate ways to use different media, they come to a consensus by observing and talking to people.

The idea of idioms of practice became important to me early on in my research because I realized that I was interviewing people with different idioms of practice all the time, despite the fact that most people I interviewed were college students at the university where I teach. This is partially a result of the ways in which I found people who were willing to chat with me about breaking up in non–face-to-face ways. I would send around an e-mail request to students in popular majors on my campus, or I would make a short announcement in my colleagues' large lecture classes asking for volunteers. I was rarely interviewing college students who talked to each other frequently. As a consequence, I found that my interviews were often with college students who had different idioms of practice. College students weren't using a piece of technology to accomplish the same kind of tasks—they didn't share the same idiom of practice. Some students use Facebook only to keep in touch with a handful of close friends; others compete on Facebook to "friend" as many people as possible. This difference in idioms of practice was true even in terms of word choices. People didn't have a shared understanding of whether to call disconnecting a "friend" link on Facebook "unfriending" or "defriending." This semantic question will probably be settled by the time this book is published. But the differences in idioms of practice went much further than questions of semantics or whether to use e-mail to communicate with a friend.

In my conversations with students, it was clear that there wasn't a widespread consensus on the social etiquette for using new technologies. For example, when I asked students in my classes who should be the first person to change their relationship status on Facebook after a breakup, people had many different ideas. One woman insisted that the person who was dumped should be the one to end things publicly on Facebook and said that everyone in her sorority thought this as well. But other students said that it was whoever reached their Facebook profile first. Others didn't think that the question of who ended the relationship on Facebook was as important as waiting a few days, that it was simply polite to wait before announcing the breakup to one's social network. There were even different beliefs about why waiting was polite. Some thought it was important to wait because some friends would want to hear the news of the breakup by phone. Others thought that people would need time to heal before dealing with the social ramifications of posting the news on Facebook. In short, people have a sense that there *are* right ways and wrong ways to change one's relationship status on Facebook after a breakup, but there is not yet any widespread consensus about what those ways might be. A large part of my interviews became uncovering the different media ideologies and different idioms of practice that people brought to breaking up in non–face-to-face ways.

One of the problems in writing this book is how rapidly and unpredictably the technologies that people use to break up with each other are changing. When I interviewed college students about Facebook in 2007 and 2008, they kept mentioning the "News Feed" and how much it affected the ways Facebook contributed to their experiences of breaking up. When people log on to their Facebook profiles, the first thing they see is the news feed, a list of all the changes to profiles in their Facebook friends' network, including any breakups announced on a Facebook profile. This changes the way in which gossip circulates among communities of active Facebook users—people now know about breakups without being told about them by a person.

Yet the news feed was a recent development. Installed on September 5, 2006, the news feed started a little less than a year before I began interviewing people. No one I talked to in 2006 about Facebook liked the news feed at first, but every student I interviewed in 2007 and 2008 found it an integral part of how they use Facebook. More important for the purposes of this book, breaking up by Facebook before the news feed was a different experience than breaking up after the news feed. Since I finished the first draft of this book, Facebook has changed the news feed again, transforming it into a live feed that provides information about how people's Facebook friends have changed their profile in "real time." This form of news feed makes the most immediate interactions on Facebook the news feed's priority. Relatively small changes in technology can transform the ways in which people circulate information and consciously manage the circulation of information. These technologies are changing so quickly that what was true when I interviewed people in 2007 and 2008 about Facebook, texting, and all the other technologies mentioned here may not be true about them by the time this is published. While the details about the technologies may change, the insights will still be relevant about how people experience newness and how they respond to being surrounded by many different idioms of practice.

To sum up, remediation, different media ideologies, different idioms of practice—all these analytical concepts point to how people are experiencing these media as new media. Because Facebook,

Pierce Inverarity Oedipa is cheating on me. I went through her phone while she was in the shower, and read the texts. What kind of a name is Mucho?
about an hour ago · Comment · Like

Oedipa Maas We have only been apart an hour, , and I keep thinking of things I want to say to you
Yesterday at 7:41pm · Comment · Like

Pierce Inverarity is rethinking his mental crush list
Wed at 9:29pm · Comment · Like

RECENT ACTIVITY

♥ Pierce went from being "in a relationship" to "single." · Comment · Like

♥ · Comment · Like

🐾 Pierce and Oedipa Maas are now friends. · Comment · Like

FIGURE 1

Sample Breakup in Facebook News Feed
This news feed is recording changes in Pierce's relationship status. People can mark their relationship status on Facebook, selecting from a menu (the options: single, in a relationship, engaged, married, it's complicated, in an open relationship, and, since August 2009, widowed). All these possibilities, except for being single, can be linked to another person's profile, a link the other person has actively chosen to accept. When Pierce announced that he was in a relationship (and Oedipa accepted), all Facebook showed was a heart.

texting, and so on are relatively new ways to communicate with each other, people haven't developed a widespread consensus on how to use the different media. People are still in the process of figuring out the social rules that might govern how to use these technologies. They are also working out how using a particular medium might affect the message sent through that medium. In asking "what makes new media new?" I am making a distinction between the fact of newness and the ways in which people understand and experience the newness of technology. Whether a piece of technology has actually been recently introduced isn't as relevant to me as how people behave and think about a piece of technology. In this book I am laying out a map for understanding how the newness of new media is socially constructed by looking at the moments when communication is most fraught and when etiquette, perhaps, is most needed.

Looking at how people break up turns out to be a useful ethnographic starting point for analyzing how people understand the newness of a medium. Breakups were moments in which everyone I interviewed would turn into a detective—they told stories about not quite knowing what was going on or not understanding why someone else was acting a certain way. They would talk directly and clearly about what someone else's use of a medium seemed to let them know about that person's intentions and actions. People would straightforwardly explain their own media ideologies as they described the technologies they and others used to end romantic relationships and friendships. Because breakups are often so emotionally charged and confusing, these are the moments in which people also begin talking with each other and evaluating how to use a particular medium. By talking, and often criticizing, the ways the breakup was accomplished, people also were laying the groundwork for shared understandings of how to use different media.

I interviewed seventy-two people for this book; almost all of them were undergraduates at the university where I teach when I interviewed them in 2007 and 2008. Five people I interviewed were older (30–50), and were married or living with their partner prior to the breakup; I indicate this when I introduce their stories. I spoke to eighteen men and fifty-four women, interviewing anyone who responded to my requests for a good story about breaking up in mediated ways that they were willing to share with me. The fact that more women responded than men probably has a lot to do with my own gender and with who felt comfortable responding to my various requests for interviews. I did not watch anyone break up with another person—all the material in this book is based on recorded interviews. The pseudonyms I use throughout the book were chosen by the people interviewed. The majority of the people spoke about their experiences breaking up with others in high school and college, so I am writing about people who were still in the process of figuring what relationships were about.

In these interviews I focused on what mediated breakups can tell us about people's media ideologies and how people experience these media as new. This is not a book about what people actually said during the breakups, or even why the breakups happened (unless new media was crucially involved—e.g., someone might be unable to stay together with their lover after he or she breaks into their Facebook account to snoop). Nor is this a how-to book—people seeking techniques for texting breakup should look elsewhere. I am writing about the intersection between disconnection and the media people use to disconnect. I look at what people say about mediated breakups as a starting point for understanding how people think about and use different media.

My interviews with college students about their breakups often undermined some of the popular stereotypes I regularly hear about how the youth of America are responding to new technologies. These stereotypes focus on how eagerly and uncritically young adults are adopting new technologies. By contrast, in my interviews, many college students were very uneasy about how the media they use shape their social interactions. They were often nostalgic for the times that were B.F. (before Facebook, launched in 2004),[5] or before texting and instant messaging. They talked about how

---

5. A term coined by Allison Faye, the real name of a student I interviewed who wanted me to mention that she came up with this phrase, which seems only reasonable.

complicated these different media made communication, focusing often on how much miscommunication was generated by a lack of intonation and other conversational cues available in face-to-face conversations. They see earlier forms of communication as easier, less prone to lead to arguments and misunderstandings. Several students I interviewed quit Facebook altogether, convinced that using Facebook had harmed their relationships. People were often ambivalent about these technologies—contrary to stereotype, they did not experience newness as an unqualified and obvious good.

At the same time, students did not use these technologies in ways that further isolated them socially. This is a common misconception that people have when I first explain my project—that the college students I interview use Facebook or instant messaging as a wholesale substitute for in-person communication. There is a popular stereotype that communication is gradually and insidiously becoming "virtual" for college students. This stereotype implies that "virtual" communication is somehow inferior and less substantive than in-person communication. This interpretation imposes a media ideology that values some forms of communication—namely, in-person communication—over any other form of communication by distinguishing between virtual and real communication in ways that not everyone does. Daniel Miller and Donald Slater are ethnographers of the Internet who warn scholars not to be the ones deciding what counts as virtual. Virtual communication, they argue, is "a social accomplishment" that sometimes accompanies a medium such as the Internet, but does not invariably do so (Miller and Slater 2000, 6). Heeding Miller and Slater, I soon realized that for the people I interviewed, Facebook, video chats, or instant messaging may be done through a computer screen, but they are not virtual. That is to say, these media are not cyberrealms distinct from other interactions, but rather Facebook communication is inextricably intertwined with every other way that they communicate. They did not understand information or meaning conveyed through Facebook or instant messaging to be "virtual," while other forms of communication conveyed "real" information or meaning.

Practically, this means that for those I interviewed, Facebook communication is but one among many ways of communicating with others. Choosing to communicate by Facebook is almost always a choice that is understood not in terms of a choice between real communication and virtual communication but rather as a choice between Facebook, phone, e-mail, instant message, or in-person communication. If two people communicated by Facebook or instant messaging, this did not necessarily mean that they only communicated by Facebook or instant messaging. Often people communicated with each other through many different media. What was important to the college students I interviewed was often not which form of communication was supposedly virtual, but rather how the medium chosen affected the kinds of conversations they thought one could have through that medium. In short, the disconnections I am talking about in this book are emphatically not the disconnections between supposedly real interactions and virtual interactions. Rather, they are disconnections between people—the endings of friendships and romances.

I am turning to the ways people disconnect as a useful ethnographic moment for examining how people experience the newness of new media. Most scholars and journalists talk about the new forms of connections that these recently invented technologies enable. Yet it isn't only new types of connections that these technologies make possible; they also make possible new forms of disconnection. Analysts often overlook some aspects of new media that I will discuss in this book because they are mainly analyzing how people connect. Turning to breakups brings into sharper focus the different idioms of practice and varied media ideologies surrounding new media. Breakups allow me a useful vantage point from which to discuss how there isn't a shared agreement about how the media should be used, what can be said through different media, or what is generally polite and not polite when using these media. The medium people use to end relationships matters. Breakups turn out to be productive sites for pointing out that people don't share the same ideas about media—ideas that shape how people use and interpret these different media. In short, how the media matter during breakups offers insights into the ways people think about different modes of communication and the ways they experience the newness of these different modes.

1

Fifty Ways to Leave Your Lover

MEDIA IDEOLOGIES AND
IDIOMS OF PRACTICE

Toward the end of the interview, just as the thirty-something Olivier and I began to say our good-byes, he told me that in the end, it was the way his wife (soon to be ex-wife) kept e-mailing his work account that was particularly distressing. They were dissolving a marriage, and this disentangling required discussion, most of which was taking place by e-mail. He was forced to create a personal folder for all the e-mails she sent to his work account, the only personal folder he had in this particular e-mail account. No matter how often he e-mailed her personal e-mail account, no matter how often he sent messages from his own personal e-mail account, she insisted on using the accounts they had both set aside for their professional lives. And when she sent these e-mails, she always sent them when she was at work. He could tell from the time attached to each e-mail. The boundaries were clear—he was no longer allowed to contact her personal account or interact with her during her personal time.

Of course this probably wasn't what bothered Olivier the most about the whole process. He was getting a divorce because his wife had sent him an e-mail out of the blue asking for a divorce and offering no reasons while he was away on a business trip. It turned out to be a nonnegotiable decision. After the two-line e-mail announcing that she wanted a divorce, she would communicate with him only by e-mail and occasional angry phone calls. She closed their joint bank accounts while he was gone, so he returned to no money and no place to stay. For weeks he had no explanation that made sense of why she wanted a divorce, although gradually he learned of another man, someone she had met at work. All the communication he had with her gave him no clear insights into why she was doing what she was doing. Knowing another man existed did not seem to explain enough for him.

She was violating all the shared order that they carefully, or even perhaps accidentally, created together—when they spoke in French or English together, when they sent e-mails to their friends from their joint e-mail account, or when they would e-mail someone from their individual personal accounts. The more Olivier detailed how divorce was affecting how he and his wife/ex-wife were using media to communicate, the more apparent it became that the couple had developed together a system for indicating that some messages were formal, some informal, some professional, and some intimate. They used e-mail accounts, phones, and different languages all to create intertwined ways of adding information to the message—a message from their joint e-mail account would signal something different than if that same message had been sent from their individual e-mail accounts. In e-mailing his work account, his wife/ex-wife was rejecting all the years of chosen habits that they had created together just through how they e-mailed. So the unseemly disorder that Olivier experienced with these e-mails to his work account—these weekly, sometimes daily, reminders of how her decisions at every level had transformed his life's plans into unwelcome chaos—captured the misery of this dissolution. Since the moment she e-mailed him to demand a divorce, Olivier explained that he felt none of his wishes were respected; sending messages only to his work e-mail was a small example that seemed to reverberate and point to all the others, beginning with the e-mail requesting a divorce.

Olivier had been using the possibilities made available by e-mail—multiple accounts—to sort his communication. His wife/ex-wife was refusing to accede to this system of classifying communication. In short, she was sending information through her choice of medium (e-mail *and* work account) as much as by the content of her messages. This double communication in the message is possible only because of Olivier's, or anyone's, media ideologies. As mentioned in the introduction, people's *media ideologies*—their beliefs about how a medium communicates and structures communication—makes a personal e-mail account different from a work e-mail account, or a text message different from a phone call. The difference often lies not in the actual message, but in people's understandings of the media. Media ideologies are responsible for the ways in which second-order information works (see chapter 4). *Second-order information* refers to the information that can guide you into understanding how particular words and statements should be interpreted.[1] One never sends a message without the message being accompanied by second-order information; that is, without indications about how the sender would like the message received.

You Can't Text Message Breakup

Media contain second-order information because of people's media ideologies, people's understandings of how e-mail, phone,

---

1. This is part, but only part, of what linguistic anthropologists have called *metapragmatics* (see Silverstein 2001).

instant messaging (IM), and other media add important information to the message. Let me give you a concrete example of when someone's media ideology got in the way of interpreting the seriousness of a text message. This is a story that Halle, an undergraduate, told me toward the end of an interview, when she suddenly remembered another story about texting. Halle and Doug had been a couple for a number of weeks. They met in a class where they both also became friends with Rianna. Rianna always struck Halle as a little bit off—she was one of those people who always seemed to say something slightly unexpected and awkward, something that made the other people in the conversation stop and scratch their heads about how to continue the conversation. As Halle and Doug started getting together, they started joking about Rianna's social gracelessness—most of this by text message. After a while, Halle began teasing Doug by text that he was secretly infatuated with Rianna. This text joking carried on for a few weeks. Then Doug texted Halle, telling her he had to break up with her because he really was in love with Rianna. This was by text, a medium that Halle had always used for joking. Texting was never a medium that Halle used to convey serious information such as "I am breaking up with you." So she couldn't understand the message at first. On the one hand, it was a complete surprise: There was no immediately prior conversation the message could be referring to. On the other hand, the only conversation they had ever had by text about Rianna was one that joked about desire. She responded as though Doug was still joking. He texted her back that he wasn't, that he was completely serious. Halle narrates:

> So then he texts me out of the blue: "I am bad at life." Which is how he talks, so I wrote back: "I know, but why?"
> "Because I wasn't kidding about Rianna this whole time."

And I was like "yeah, right, hahaha."

And he says: "no really, I wasn't kidding."

[Halle interrupts recounting the texts to point out] These are all text messages.

[He continues] "No really, I really like her."

I was like—wait, are we still kidding? That is what I said, "Are we still kidding?"

And he said, "No, I talked to one of my best girlfriends from home, and she said that it's not fair to keep seeing you the whole time I am thinking about her."

And I am like—what is going on? These are *text messages* about something that we have been joking about, and I have no idea what is going on. I am completely out of the loop.... So that was it. I haven't talked to him since.

The second-order communication—what Halle understands it means to communicate this kind of information by text—seems to her to be at odds with what the words of the text message were about. For Halle, the medium was at odds with the message. She had to do some follow-up investigation by asking him if he was kidding so that she could decide what interpretation she should finally give to the messages they were exchanging. In the end, Halle decided that he had behaved badly by communicating this to her by text, so badly that she stopped communicating with him entirely.

How Halle understands texting as a medium shapes the ways in which she responds to Doug's message. The texting was supposed to give second-order disclaimers to the message—carried along with the message was this imaginary additional frame urging the receiver to understand that nothing said in this medium is serious because texting is not a serious medium. Halle feels that Doug violates this tacit assumption—he says serious things in a medium that she considers appropriate only for the most casual and joking of conversations. Let's not forget that Doug tells Halle that he wants to break up with her for Rianna, a woman she doesn't respect and finds off-putting. This too is part of the story. But it is Halle's media ideology that in her own account affects how she decides to treat Doug afterward. She decides not to keep communicating with someone who texts this kind of information, and thus in her mind behaves badly. When Doug tried to get back together repeatedly (by texting, not through face-to-face communication), she turned him down. I am not saying Halle was wrong or right. Instead, I am pointing to how important media ideologies can be in shaping how people actually interpret the messages they receive. Content isn't everything; media ideologies matter.

Sometimes when people talk about ideologies, they talk about beliefs that mystify, that keep someone from understanding how things truly are. The term *ideology* does not have that connotation for me. Media ideologies are not true or false. An e-mail conversation is not, in its essence, more formal than an instant-message conversation—or less honest or spontaneous, or more calculated. But some people *believe* that e-mail is more formal, more dishonest, and more calculated, and this affects the ways they send and interpret e-mail messages. Understanding people's media ideologies can give insights into how utterances are received, and why people choose to reply in particular ways. But studying media ideologies will not give insights into what is *really* being communicated as opposed to what people believe is being communicated. It is not an analytical tool for discerning truth or reality; instead, it is but one analytical tool for understanding the ways in which all communication is socially constructed and socially interpreted. Understanding media ideologies is central to understanding how communication happens, especially now when there are so many possible media from which to choose.

The "How" of Breaking Up

Why do people talk about the medium of a breakup? In my interviews, I learned about people's media ideologies from their emotionally charged stories about endings. I was finding out about how they thought the media that were used affected the communication when the conversations were all about love or desire and its loss. People were talking about appropriateness all the time, about why one medium might be appropriate or inappropriate for ending a relationship. Sometimes I talked to people about how certain technologies had contributed to ending relationships; for example, how sharing passwords had, in retrospect, become the first step in destroying a relationship. I talked to college students about ending friendships as well, about the differences between ending romantic relationships and ending friendships. What I now know about people's media ideologies is intimately linked to what they said about different media as a means for communicating about ending relationships.

Talking about how people choose to end a relationship may be a common American way to talk about breakups. When I was discussing this project with another anthropologist, Ray McDermott, in a tea shop in Palo Alto, he recalled when he and his students had interviewed Americans about being in a family in the early 1980s. He said that when people talked about divorce, many focused on how things were said, what words were used. At the time, there weren't so many media to choose from—people would talk in person, call on a landline or write a letter. Ray said that people tended to describe their sense of outrage, injustice, and grievance in terms of *how* someone had ended the relationship, not *that* the relationship was ending. The resentment that people were willing to voice about ending relationships all revolved around the form of the ending. When they would narrate how the relationship ended, they would focus on what was said. In my interviews, this held true as well. Turning to the media used is just an extension of a U.S. tendency to discuss breakups by describing the way breakups took place.

When people focus on the "how" of a breakup, particular aspects of a medium become important—whether it is too formal or too informal, whether it allows for intonation, conversational turn-taking, circulation of the breakup text, explanation, and so on. In my interviews, some media were generally acknowledged to be deficient in one way or another. When people explained to me the problems with texting, as I mentioned in the introduction, they often focused on how brief text messages had to be. Breakups should ideally be adequately explained, and how much can one actually say in 160 characters? In addition, some people insisted, text messages were for deciding only the most casual of arrangements such as when one should meet for dinner or who else might want to go to the movies. For these people, text messaging is too informal for something as serious or important as a breakup.

Formality and Informality: Assessing Media

The formality or informality of a medium depends on people's media ideologies; there is nothing inherent in a medium to make it more formal or informal than any other medium. The kind of informality people agree to attribute to a particular medium, such as texting, will shape when it is appropriate to use that medium. While text messages might be too informal for a breakup, they often had the right level of informality for starting to flirt with someone. Women insisted to me that if they met someone who was interested in them, they would exchange phone numbers, but only to text each other. Calling would express too much interest; calling would be too forward a move. But texting was considered to carry low enough stakes that one could begin an exchange with the right level of ambiguity, unclear whether the exchange is about friendship or desire. As Summer suggested in her interview, discussing the text message she saved that a cute man had sent her a half hour after their first conversation: "The good thing about texting is that it's that nice in-between between calling and not doing anything. It's not so desperate."

It is this very casualness that makes texting a problematic medium for breaking up. One connects to someone initially using texting because people presume that texting reveals so little about the depth or seriousness of one's emotions. As a result, it is hardly appropriate as a medium for breaking up. What is caution in one's choice of media in the initial contact becomes cowardice at the end.

Texting's brevity and informality also affects the ways texting is actually used in a breakup. Here I want to distinguish between media ideology and practice. When people told me about their media ideologies of texting, they would stress how inappropriate texting was as a medium for breaking up.[2] Sometimes, however, when they talked about how text messages actually played a role in their breakups, I got a different sense of how text messages functioned. People would tell me about choosing to start text-message fights on purpose, ones that sometimes, but not always, led to breakups. People would prefer text-message fights because, as Rose explained to me,

---

2. Even the one person I interviewed who thought I was clearly very old-fashioned for suggesting that texting was not acceptable as a breakup medium also told me in detail about how casual many of her relationships were. In this case, part of what seemed to help texting be so acceptable was the ways in which its informality helped to emphasize her relationships' casualness.

the recipient would focus his or her entire attention on what you were saying by text and would have to respond to that message. Rose compared this with face-to-face fights:

> I feel like for the most part in [face-to-face] fights, women, like I said, scream at men, and the men nod like this [demonstrates how the men stare off into space] and nod like this, and [the woman says] "oh, you said this" and you scream at them more for saying it, and they nod. And at the end of the fight you feel better and they just let it go and everything is okay.

And yet, the woman never really knows whether the nodding man was actually listening to her. But, as she explained, with a text message, the man has to pay attention to the words, and he has to respond to what the woman is saying. Texts, she went on to say, were *always* answered. You could delete an e-mail or a voice mail, but texts require both attention and a response.

Because of this, some people used text messages to begin the breakup ritual. Texting "I want to breakup" in some cases was only the mediated version of the face-to-face utterance: "We have to talk." The possibility of a breakup is promised but not definite. Instead, texting a wish to breakup in the early evening sometimes ensured frantic phone calls or long face-to-face conversations until six in the morning. A text message's very informality, however, meant uttering the desire to breakup by text might not be taken seriously as a desire. Much more conversational work would have to occur to make the desire become fact. Several people thought that a text-message breakup wouldn't result in a breakup. Cole said, "If I texted my girlfriend 'I want to break up with you' I think she wouldn't take it seriously. She would probably laugh."

I have been discussing the dilemmas of using too informal a medium for breaking up, but too formal a medium can also be a problem. Only one person told me about being dumped by letter—and this on cream stationery written with what she suspected was a quill pen. In this case, it was the very formality of the letter that bothered Eleanor. She knew the breakup was probably coming. They had lived in the same dorm, and as long as they primarily communicated face-to-face, all seemed to go well. He wouldn't text her and when she texted him, his phone was often turned off. For the most part, there was no reason to communicate any other way but face to face—they lived in the same place. But when they went home for the summer, four hours away from each other, their communication started to go sour. They kept arguing by phone. So Eleanor thought a breakup was likely, but did not expect it by cream stationery. She described in detail, with a mixture of horror and amusement, the seriousness of tone, the surprise of getting such a formal document in the mail. "Who does that anymore?" she kept asking. She would have much preferred a phone call.

Cream stationery aside, the medium that most undergraduates described to me as formal was e-mail. As I mentioned in my introduction, people's media ideologies about e-mail reveal a generation gap in the ways people understand technology. Even undergraduates who were unhappy with the ways in which new media were changing people's communication,[3] would describe e-mail as the closest regular form of communication that they had to letters; that is, to more traditional forms of communication. By contrast with all the other media they used regularly, e-mail seemed the most formal, used to communicate with employers, professors, parents, and grandparents. One student, who wanted the pseudonym

---

3. Many of my interviews had a strong undercurrent of nostalgia for the way communication used to be, before texting, e-mail, instant messaging, Facebook, and so on.

Gunslinger, chatted with me about what he thought about e-mail, distinguishing between handwritten letters and e-mail:

[In e-mail] Every letter looks the same, they are identical. I push the button, but it wasn't my hand making the note. But it is incredibly helpful and it's shrinking the world, and it is so much easier to communicate, blah blah blah, all those wonderful things. So in that sense, e-mail is the best tool. You can clearly think out what you are trying to say as long as you don't write an angry e-mail. But you could just as easily write an angry letter. And as soon as you send it, you regret it, and you try to jam your hand into the blue box, but you can't get it, just like you can't unsend an e-mail. So those two, in that vein they are very similar, in that they both still have their problems, but since we have been writing letters as long as we have been around, we know how to approach them better. Whereas instant messaging, and texting, they are fairly new technologies so there really is no etiquette.

For the Gunslinger, e-mail and letters gradually became almost interchangeable as he thought about the etiquette challenges each presented. Other people his age with whom I spoke would also quickly equate letters and e-mails, viewing them as interchangeably formal.

Older people, by contrast, viewed e-mail as informal and described the way its informality affected communication. Noah, a professor of physics in his forties at my university, shared his perspective that e-mail was not similar to letters at all but far more linked to spoken communication:

Because e-mail is so connected to oral communication, we feel like we are saying something quite well when we type it out. And then you can go back to it a day later and you realize—oh, this really wasn't nearly as well-written as I thought it would be, which is not as much an experience I have with sort of conventional typing. The ways

I know it is linked to oral communications is (a) I notice how often I am saying things out loud as I type them on e-mail, which is not something I do with normal word-processing and (b) the number of times I make phonetic spelling errors. What did I do just a couple days ago? It would have been potentially embarrassing, I spelled out the word that sounded like what I was saying, but I really meant a different word entirely. I don't know if it was "through" or "threw." The fact that I have seen those kinds of errors written by brilliant scholars makes me realize that this is something about e-mail. People make grammatical and spelling errors in e-mail that they would never make on a memo they were typing on the exact same keyboard.

E-mail is a medium in which media ideologies are most sharply differentiated along generational lines, with people of Noah's generation viewing e-mail as informal and people of the Gunslinger's generation seeing e-mail almost as formal a medium as one can have, second only to a letter.

Up until now, I have been describing how people's media ideologies determine the formality of medium. There is nothing intrinsically formal or informal about a particular medium; it all depends on what its users decide is formal or informal. However, the relative formality of a medium is but one small aspect of how media ideologies affect people's breakup experiences. Breakups make people focus on other ways different media might affect communication as well. For example, while people's e-mail ideologies tend to center around the ways in which they compare e-mail to letters, people's instant-messaging ideology, by contrast, centers around the way instant messaging resembles face-to-face conversations.

Is It Like Face-to-Face Conversation?

People are constantly developing their media ideologies through comparison, attributing certain qualities to one medium because they are tacitly contrasting it to other media. Thus when people compared texting with instant messaging, they would talk about how texting was ever-present and too informal, while instant messaging could offer a textual representation of spoken conversation. When faced with a hypothetical question such as "Which is a better medium for breaking up?", people would talk about how instant messaging allows for conversational turn-taking, how people always respond to each other in real-time. People could take hours to text a response, and one never knew when it would arrive. An instant messaging response, by contrast, one could see being typed. Sometimes people mentioned that they could get information about the other person's state of mind by the speed and rhythm of their typing, once they knew the person well enough. In addition, instant messaging affords the possibility for explanation and a dialogue in which the person being dumped can ask "why?" One woman, who requested the pseudonym Duae Vultae, largely preferred to break up by instant message. She explained why in the following way:

> *Duae Vultae:* [Most people think] breaking up in person is ideal. But I just think that when it comes to breaking up with someone, if I am sure that I want to break up with someone, then the best way is to do it through other means.
>
> *Ilana:* So what do you try?
>
> *Duae Vultae:* I usually just go on instant messenger, and I make it as clear and straightforward as possible. And I leave no room for doubts. Because when you see someone in person, it's harder to bring it up. And once you do bring it up, you are going to be affected by how that person responds to it. You will feel bad. And then you might change your mind based on how that person responds, if they start crying or something like that. But then, through instant messaging, you will just say it, and you won't see

how they react....Most people think it's very harsh. Somehow it never bothered my conscience that it was just done with. It's probably better for them too. I just don't like to drag out a relationship that I have determined to end.

Ilana: So let me ask you, you are choosing instant messaging. And you have other choices. What is it about instant messaging?

Duae Vultae: Other choices, maybe phone? I could call them. That also makes it more difficult—talking. You know, talking makes it more personal. And then, if I text, its just, I don't know, then I feel like I still need to leave room for a little bit of explanation and text messaging, that would take a long time to respond back. So, or e-mail, now e-mail—I like the immediate response. With instant messaging you can do that. And if they get upset, you can just sign off, and okay, it's done. But then through e-mail, you have to wait to see....If I am absolutely certain about the breakup, then it's instant messaging.

When people objected to instant messaging, they often pointed to the way in which IM might not be enough like spoken conversation. One student in a class of mine said that the problem with instant messaging was that you never knew if you were the only person they were talking to at that moment. Because this is on a computer screen, someone could be breaking up with one person and hooking up with another at the same time. In short, instant messaging could not guarantee that someone's whole attention was on the person they were typing to. Technically this is also true of e-mail, Facebook, or text messages. But it is the ways that people talk about instant messaging and how similar it is to face-to-face conversations that also makes the differences that they notice between these two ways of communicating more of a problem.

Another discomfort people had with instant messaging is that someone could simply end the conversation abruptly and without any forewarning. When people do this in face-to-face conversations, there are bodily movements that give some indication that this may be about to happen, and perhaps some clues as to why someone has chosen to end a conversation. By IM, there are no such nonverbal clues, so this ending is perceived as much more abrupt. Olivia told me a story about how her eighth-grade boyfriend had responded to her desire to breakup over IM by simply logging off.

> This is when instant messenger was a big part of my life—away messages told about your state of mind. You would put up the quote of a song, and it told if you were happy or sad....I had this boyfriend and it was eighth grade. He asked me out through his friend, we talked online, and we hung out, like, once, and then I got freaked out. I am not ready for this. I broke up with him online [by IM]. And then, of course, it's like that is the equivalent of deactivating [Facebook], is the person who signs off without saying anything. It's like "oh my god, are they going to go kill themselves, did they go to cry, or are they pissed off, and they don't care?"...I remember what I said, and my heart was pounding. And then he just signed off, and that was his response. I was good friends with his friends, and they told me that he was upset and everything. And he wasn't online for a few days...so I was worried about him.

Signing off instant messaging without announcing he was going felt far too vague for Olivia. She was fourteen at the time, and this was one of the first times she had ever ended a relationship, so she did not have many past experiences to help place his behavior in context. And his actions were too ambiguous for her to evaluate what might be the consequences of her desire to end the relationship. In short, she needed more information about how his media ideology and his practice coincided to interpret his actions.

I have been describing some of the media ideologies at play when people break up with each other (and there are many more), in part to clarify what it means to analyze new media from an ethnographic or anthropological perspective. I could discuss the ways I think a medium functions—whether texting ensures more of an immediate answer than instant messaging or e-mail, and how that might affect a breakup—but that would be an interpretation based on my own assumptions and experiences with technology. People develop understandings of how media functions based on their own practices and conversations they have with the people they know, as well as the stories they hear and see through the media.[4] Their media ideologies always managed to surprise me, and make me think about the technologies we were talking about in a new way. People are unpredictable, one can't tell without asking and observing what media ideologies they hold, and how their beliefs shape their practices. Some people I talked to thought that a text message always required a response; others had no problem ignoring text messages. Whether texts required response or could be ignored was part of a person's media ideology; it had nothing to do with the cell phone equipment. In short, one should not presume to know the media ideologies that accompany a particular technology in advance without asking a person many questions to determine what his or her media ideologies and practices are.

Dating People with Different Media Ideologies

There is a corollary to what I am presenting here—people don't necessarily share the same media ideologies. Being American, or a white middle-class American undergraduate is not enough

---

4. Upon hearing about my project, many people responded by telling me about the *Sex and the City* episode in which Berger breaks up with Carrie Bradshaw on a Post-it note.

information to predict with any degree of accuracy what your media ideology will be. I realized as I interviewed more and more people that not only did people have different media ideologies, but they were often dating people with different media ideologies. This would occasionally make the breakups more difficult. One person might think a text message was a perfectly acceptable way to start a breakup conversation—a conversation that they just assumed would drift to phone or face-to-face conversation before the end of the night. The other person might be horrified to get the message by text message and refuse to speak to their now ex-lover ever again. When I began interviewing people, I expected some variety in how they understood the ways that media affected messages. After all, because these media ideologies are *ideologies,* they are always multiple, locatable, positioned, and contested. What I didn't expect was how multiple and how contested all these media ideologies would be.

In my interviews, people often described having to guess what other people's media ideologies might be to interpret why they were using a particular medium to accomplish a certain communicative task. For example, on Facebook, you can send a public message by posting to someone's wall so anyone in their Facebook network can know the content of the message, the author, and the time it was sent. With a private Facebook message, only the addresser and addressee can see the message. So Joe invites Jen to go bowling via a Facebook wall post; should Jen consider this a date? Why is Joe sending this message so publicly—to make it less of a date (that is more casual) or more of a date (warning other people who might be interested in Jen that he, Joe, was pursuing her)? This particular utterance drove Jen to Joe's profile for any insight into how Joe understands and uses Facebook. And once one starts dating, as many readers may have discovered, regular intimate contact does not necessarily shed comprehensive light on how another person communicates or interprets the media through which they are communicating.

The fact that people don't necessarily share media ideologies means that they don't necessarily agree on how one should use particular media, either to connect or disconnect with each other. Yet being able to interpret other people's media ideologies with any accuracy can affect how your conversations will flow. As I mentioned before, if two people agree that a text message is too informal a medium for breaking up, they might decide that a text message fight containing the stated desire to break up should not be taken seriously. Only a face-to-face encounter following the fight can best resolve the argument, and might potentially lead to reconciliation. But if one person decides that texting is so informal a medium that any breakup utterance performed within this medium is unconscionable (as Halle did in the story toward the beginning of this chapter), then rather than having an imminent reconciliation, a breakup has just taken place. In short, it is not just how you think about a medium, it is how you reflexively engage with the medium given what you think about it.

And Then She Texted Me

Media ideologies are central to explaining one of the striking features of the stories people told me: People *always* mentioned which medium was used whenever they recounted a conversation. As people of all ages told me breakup stories, they tended to tell me not only the sequence of events, who said what and when, but they also always mentioned the media in which each conversation or message took place. They would point out whenever there was a switch in medium, letting me know whenever the narrated conversational exchanges switched from phone to texting, for example. At first, I suspected that the people I was interviewing were generously humoring me—they knew I was interested in communicative technology and so they were willing to seamlessly mark its presence when they narrated their breakup conversations in an interview. But once I started paying attention, it became clear that mentioning the medium is a relatively typical feature of contemporary American breakup narratives. All my friends constantly link the utterance with its communicative medium, and many breakup narratives featured on radio shows or television or posted on blogs and other Web sites do as well. Here is a typical example of what I am describing from the Dumpedster Web site[5]—this was posted in May 2003:

> Alexis asked me out via the Internet. She was cute, hip, and a scientist. We went on five dates, but each one seemed like a first date. She let me kiss her, but never really responded. Conversation was so-so. Oh, and on the second date, I met her dad. We had plans for Memorial Day, but she never called me, and didn't respond to my voice-mail....The next day, I got an e-mail apologizing for blowing me off and saying "I needed to give myself a hall pass not to call" and "I don't want to be in a relationship right now."

The Internet, voice mail, e-mail, and hall passes all appear in this narrative. In their stories, people are tracking the media through which breakups are unfolding. Why do they do this? What work is being done when people retell what was said or typed, while constantly reminding the audience what medium was used?

I'll begin to answer by pointing out something that readers may have been wondering about. Saying or writing "I want to break

---

5. The website Dumpedster (www.dumpedster.com) is now defunct.

up" is not necessarily effective: suggesting breaking up does not actually result in breaking up. People are often ambivalent about breaking up—one person may want to break up more than the other, or both people may be uncertain. Clarity on this front can seem like an elusive achievement. It turns out that the medium through which "I want to breakup" is uttered contributes to its effectiveness. Louise, who was in her late twenties, had been in a seven-year relationship that had begun to contain many ambiguous conversations about whether it should continue or not. These conversations went on for months, but Louise and her significant other were still together. Finally her significant other e-mailed her that he wanted to end the relationship. When Louise reflected on the breakup, it was the e-mail that she focused on, calling it cowardly, and joking months later that she should have refused the breakup and instead waited for the text message. In fact, after the e-mail, she stopped all contact with him. She considered performing a breakup over e-mail so indicative of his personal failings that she didn't want to continue interacting.

Before I began this research, I thought that a fairly typical response to being dumped by the wrong medium might be to refuse any further contact with the person ending the relationship. Even the popular fictional "Text Message Breakup" Youtube video (http://www.youtube.com/watch?v=XcidD2HFK8M) depicts this response to a breakup e-mail or breakup text as the predictable response. A woman raps about the social costs her boyfriend/ex-boyfriend will now pay—namely, never sleeping with anyone else—because he has breached social norms by breaking up by text-message after a two-year relationship, the chorus being "You don't text message breakup." Yet as I mentioned earlier, for some college students, a text-message breakup just indicates that the phone calls or instant messaging will now start. For these people, a text-message breakup is rarely accomplished solely by texting; other media would almost immediately be called upon for this task. Texting a breakup may only be the beginning of the ritual of breaking up, and in some sense the warning shot across the bow. Just because you say you want to break up doesn't mean that you are actually going to break up. You could be having one of many fights or be about to redefine some of the terms of the relationship, but ending the relationship is not a given.

Facebook plays an ambiguous role in how it facilitates breaking up. Sometimes it creates a sharply defined ending. For Leslie, the Facebook breakup served the same function as e-mail did in my first interview. Leslie checked her Facebook profile late in the day, and found out that she was suddenly single. In fact, she learned that her boyfriend, now ex-boyfriend, had a new girlfriend through the news feed that flashes on as soon as one logs on. And then she noticed that her profile had changed, that he was no longer listed as the person she was in a relationship with. This was a Facebook breakup that was immediately effective. And she said ruefully that because of the news feed, everyone else knew before she did. In this case, the medium helped determine whether indicating "I want to break up" becomes effective over time.

But in other cases the news feed also reveals to people how unstable Facebook claims can be—that is, how unstable a person's single status can be. While some people will claim that a breakup isn't official until it is "Facebook official," just because it has become Facebook official doesn't mean that it has taken. People will waiver—one day they announce on Facebook that the relationship is in trouble, the next day they announce that they are back together. A community's first indication that a relationship is in trouble is often the rapid changes to a Facebook relationship status. So Facebook is a glimpse into other people's disconnections, but a glimpse that tantalizes instead of satisfying. And what is often unknown is whether the breakup is going to take—is the news feed recording a breakup saga or a narrative of renewing commitment, of near dissolution narrowly averted? Which kind of story will the breakup statement on Facebook eventually contribute to when the events become a story that circulates?

I want to suggest that because people don't share the same media ideologies, especially about new media, part of what someone is doing by marking every medium in their story is tracing the detective work they had to do to determine which genre of story this narrative was going to become as it unfolded. The interactions might be a relationship fight leading to renewed commitment, or they might signal a breakup. Each person's intentions are unclear, and can only be retroactively guessed at by seeing how what they say and what they do align. One of the clues that people focus on as they try to guess in hindsight what was going on is the medium that each person uses. Their choice of media can be read as formal or informal, enabling intonation or devoid of intonation, allowing for conversational turn-taking or preventing it, public or private, and so on. By recounting the medium used, people can gain some insight into other people's media ideologies, and often people realize that these media ideologies are not shared in the moment of a breakup. The question "Why would anyone text that?" is a good indication that people are not sharing the same media ideology about texting.

Idioms of Practice

People's media ideologies contribute to why they mention the medium of a message as they tell the stories of their breakups. They are explaining the message—people's media ideologies ensure that the same sentences are interpreted and experienced differently when read on a computer screen or on a cell phone. There is another reason, though, that marking the medium contributes to the detective work of trying to understand a breakup: People have what I am calling different *idioms of practice,* a term I mentioned in the introduction. Groups of friends, classes, workers in an office will develop together their own ways of using media to communicate with each other. Sometimes they realize that their way of using a medium is distinctive, that it marks them as different from other people. Sometimes they don't perceive that their use of a medium is unique until some miscommunication or unexpected way someone was communicating made it clear (often unpleasantly clear) that others have different idioms of practice.

Two main reasons emerged from the interviews to explain why there are so many idioms of practice with new media right now, why people keep discovering that there isn't a general consensus about how or if to use different media to accomplish different communicative tasks, such as breaking up. First, because these are new media, people haven't had time to develop a widespread consensus about how to use a medium, especially for relatively rare communicative tasks such as breaking up. As Lisa Gitelman, a historian of media, points out, things we now take for granted about the telephone took a while to be established.

> Inventing, promoting, and using the first telephones involved lots of self-conscious attention to telephony. But today, people converse through the phone without giving it a moment's thought. The technology and all of its supporting protocols (that you answer "Hello?" and that you pay the company, but also standards like touch-tones and twelve-volt lines) have become self-evident as the result of social processes, including the habits associated with other, related media. (Gitelman 2006, 5–6)

As Gitelman explains, much of what we take for granted about older communicative technology like the telephone had to be

FIGURE 2
Choosing a Relationship Status
When you want to indicate that you are no longer in a relationship on Facebook, you have two choices. You can either delete your relationship status entirely or you can choose the "single" option from the Facebook relationship status menu.

established. Saying "hello" was a phrase Thomas Edison had to invent and convince others to use instead of Alexander Graham Bell's suggestion—"ahoy."

Second, communicating with these new media can present social dilemmas that people have to solve—and will often try to figure out with their friends. I am not blaming the designers of these media. You can cancel your relationship on Facebook by changing your relationship status on Facebook. Facebook asks you directly if you want to cancel the relationship. I don't think that the people designing Facebook are at fault when someone can't bear to press "cancel," and so has to turn to her roommate to help her click. People's communicative needs are so varied and unpredictable that they are constantly facing the question of how best to use a particular medium given its structure and their media ideologies. And in these moments, as they develop strategies for communicating to solve specific problems (such as having someone else press "confirm"), they are fashioning their own idioms of practice.

I have talked earlier about people's different answers to the question: Who changes the relationship status on Facebook after a breakup (and thus in 2008 forced the other person to face the broken-heart icon on their profile)? The fact that when I ask a group of undergraduates I always get so many different answers suggests that there are many different idioms of practice, and no shared consensus. Even people's choice of words for certain activities indicates that people have different idioms of practice. In media stories about quitting Facebook (i.e., closing your Facebook account), journalists and bloggers often call this practice "Facebook suicide." No one I interviewed used this phrase; they tended to call it "deactivating" their Facebook account. When I introduced them to the term Facebook suicide, they sometimes responded with great glee. Facebook suicide, after all, is catchier.

Deleting Facebook Friends: Different Idioms of Practice

In my interviews with college students, Facebook emerged as the primary medium that people used in very different ways and often they did not seem to have a shared consensus on how to use the medium. This is partially because Facebook is more recent (2004) than the other mediums that college students were using to end relationships. Ending Facebook friendships turned out to be another instance in my interviews in which people had different idioms of practice. A person can cancel a Facebook friendship by clicking on an X near the Facebook friend's name. Once the person clicks to cancel the friendship, Facebook asks: "Remove friend? Are you sure you want to remove Harry Potter as a friend? This cannot be undone. Harry Potter will not be notified." You then have to confirm that you do indeed want to cancel the Facebook friendship. Some people said they never defriended anyone on Facebook. As the Gunslinger puts it:

> If someone angers me, I just don't talk to them. It is so trivial to have them no longer associated with you on the Internet. I mean, I am trying to put this in a more base term—when you look at someone, it won't say friends in common—the Gunslinger and "so and so." So many people are going: "They're friends? I thought they didn't like each other." But what is the point?

The Gunslinger, and others, thought that Facebook friends means so little that defriending was an excessive act of hostility. Intriguingly, other people had regular bouts of defriending friends, and gave exactly the same reason for these purges: that Facebook friends don't really matter. Rosie described how she regularly goes through and defriends some of her Facebook friends:

Ilana: What about defriending?

Rosie: I just do it. I had so many friends on Facebook, and I didn't even really know them all. I mean, I knew them, but they weren't of any real importance to me. So I went through a defriending purge, spree actually. And I went from 700 friends and I have like 56 now.

Ilana: When did you do this?

Rosie: Over the last year, probably. I went through one [purge] where I deleted all the fake Facebook profiles, like Bruce

Buckeye, Brad Pitt, that kind of thing. Then I started going through high school, people I don't talk to from high school. There are a lot.

Ilana: Did you get any comments about this?

Rosie: No, I never had anybody try to re-friend me. So I am guessing that they didn't even realize that I did it. Or they just didn't care, in which case I didn't need to be friends with them on Facebook anyway. My rule now is that I periodically go through my friends list and I ask: "okay, have I talked to this person in the last couple of months? No. Okay. Should I get rid of them? Probably." There are some people that I don't talk to on a regular basis that I keep on there. For the most part, if I don't talk to them on a regular basis, or interact with them in real life, I probably don't keep those friends on Facebook or MySpace.

Both Rosie and the Gunslinger are addressing the same social dilemma: how they should best maintain a social network whose members have privileged access to their profile and often circulate too much information (people's news feed could be too packed with information about people they don't know well or care about).[6] Some people felt that to be a Facebook friend was so minimal a link that to deny someone this link was especially rude—the metaphorical equivalent of refusing to say "how are you doing?" to a friend of a friend, someone you barely know and pass on the street. Others do not want to clutter their network (and news feed) with people they don't know well.

Some people broadcast their personal information so often that even reluctant defrienders will cut the link. Paul, who rarely

6. At the time that I was interviewing, Facebook did not allow you to choose whether or not a Facebook friend's information would appear in your news feed. This changed in 2009.

defriends on Facebook, decided to remove someone from another networking site, his livejournal blog network (www.livejournal. com) because she wrote so much that his livejournal page was filled only with her entries and no one else's.

> *Paul:* So this was on livejournal. This wasn't on Facebook, this was on livejournal. It's basically a public diary…a blog that works a little differently because you can basically create communities. It was a big thing in high school, a big big thing in high school. And when you write something down, you put up a post if you are friends with someone. Then on your friends' page, your post will be there. She would post all the time, like maybe five times a day. And it is supposed to be like once a day, maybe three times a week. That sort of daily or less ballpark. She would post five times a day! So my friends' page would be cluttered with all her posts. I still liked her as a friend, but I couldn't have that many things cluttering up my friends' page. So I took her off, we aren't livejournal friends anymore.
>
> *Ilana:* Did you tell her?
>
> *Paul:* I don't think so. We were in drum line [in the band] together. We weren't close enough to talk all the time. We were within the same friends' circle, which was part of the reason why I didn't want her cluttering up my friends' page. You know, friend of a friend. So I don't think I actually told her that. I am not sure that she knows. I imagine that she knows. At the same time, she has five hundred livejournal friends.

Paul put a lot of thought into figuring out whether or not this might offend her. He decided that they didn't know each other all that well, that this wasn't a violation of tacit friendship expectations. He also decided that she was unlikely to value him all that highly either, given how many livejournal friends she had. He hoped that one less link out of five hundred links surely could not matter *that* much to her, but this was all guesswork on Paul's part.

Of course sometimes people do defriend each other out of anger. It is even more of a statement when there are different idioms of practice involved, when someone defriends another who believes that a Facebook friend is a minimal acknowledgment of a social connection, and thus would never defriend anyone. This happened to Sadie, who would never defriend anyone, as she explains in response to my question: How did she know she had been defriended?

> *Sadie:* She had already decided a week before, two weeks, maybe three weeks that she didn't want to be my friend, but she didn't tell me in person. So not everyone is like this particular person. But it was surreal.
>
> *Ilana:* How did you know that it was weeks earlier?
>
> *Sadie:* I am just guessing. It could have been the day before, it could have been three weeks before. Because I hadn't had an occasion to message her. And her profile hadn't changed, maybe her profile hadn't changed in a couple of weeks. Since that is another way that you find out. It was very unsettling. I was sort of like "wait, what? Did you seriously defriend me?" And at that point I was angry, because she was disagreeing with me, but she was still talking to me an hour beforehand. And I had had other conversations with her. She wasn't super-friendly, and she was sort of strange. I didn't really notice it until I saw this and knew that she didn't want to be my friend anymore.

In this case, the fact that the people involved had different idioms of practice surrounding Facebook friending and defriending made this defriending meaningful and painful.

I interviewed someone else for whom friending or defriending had little to do with being acquaintances and much more to do with how people circulate knowledge. Noelle told me that when she was curious about someone on Facebook, she would request to be their friend. They tended to say yes; people often friended other people they suspected that they vaguely knew. She would then look at their profile, figure out what she wanted to know, and then promptly defriend them.

> *Ilana:* How do you decide whether to friend someone or not?
>
> *Noelle:* Oh, sometimes if I want to be nosy, I want to look at the wall, but if you can't, I will friend somebody, and see what I have to see, and then delete them as a friend. I do that all the time, if I want to look at their pictures or something, just to be nosy, and then I just defriend them.

I must admit, when Noelle told me this, my first thought was, "Well, that's a different idiom of practice." No one else I interviewed would friend and defriend quite like that. Several of the people I had already interviewed would be horrified at the idea of someone doing this, but just as many might wish that they had thought of it themselves.

The wide range of idioms of practice I was encountering in interviews occasionally made for some awkward interview moments. When I was talking to college students about their use of communicative technology, I didn't want to introduce them to new techniques; I just wanted to find out what they did. But I would occasionally, to my surprise, find myself explaining or unwittingly warning people about others' practices. For example, I often asked students about fake Facebook profiles, which I had first learned about from one interviewee as a technique to find out who one's ex-lover is now dating without revealing that you want to know. In short, a fake Facebook profile can be an asset in one's Facebook stalking (more on Facebook stalking in chapter 4). But sometimes students were surprised to find out from my questions that fake Facebook profiles existed that weren't obvious jokes. In this, and other similar moments, I unwittingly stumbled across the fact that I was interviewing college students with numerous idioms of practice.

I have been trying to write from a nonjudgmental standpoint on people's various idioms of practice because I believe that one person's media ideology and use of technology is no better or worse than another's. This is the privilege and obligation of analyzing people's practices. Being a good analyst of others' practices involves accepting the validity of others' perspectives. This isn't a stance you can easily or comfortably take when you are constantly communicating with people with different idioms of practice. As an analyst, I was encountering people's different uses of technology as stories, not as practices that affected me personally. I am able to analyze and write without judging other people's behavior as ethical—a luxury that people in the thick of things don't have. It is not surprising that in my interviews, people were constantly making moral judgments. They felt strongly that some ways of using technology were wrong. For example, in response to my question about what Facebook's relationship status option "it's complicated" might mean, Keith said:

> Dumb! Dumb! Why? I don't know…like I just feel like it is so trivial and so childish. What are you telling people like when you put that up there? No, I am not interested in your advances because I kind of got this thing going on with someone. Well then, just like…just remove it, just take it all off. And if people are unsure, you should be enough of an adult…you should have enough social skills to be able to give someone a sign that like 'hey, that's really sweet of you—not interested, got some stuff going on.' You need to do it through 'it's complicated' on Facebook? Really?

Not everyone I interviewed was as outspoken or funny in their critique as Keith, but most people had strong senses of what is an appropriate or inappropriate use of technology.

As people develop their solutions to social quandaries with their friends, they also are developing ethical expectations, senses of right and wrong technological uses. Just as there aren't widely shared idioms of practice, or media ideologies, there also aren't widely shared ethical evaluations of media use. What people are trying to figure out are the ethics of how to end the relationship as they break up with people and then tell their friends stories about their breakups.

How people understand the media they use shapes the ways they will use it. As a result, determining people's media ideologies is crucial when you are trying to figure out the ways that people communicate through different technologies. Often, people take for granted their own assumptions about how a medium shapes the information transmitted. They don't always realize that their way of using communicative technology is but one of many ways, that what they focus on as important features of a medium may not be generally held to be the important features. This is less often the case when the communicative technologies have been around for a while. Over time, people's practices can change from being idioms to widely accepted practices. When media is relatively new, the medium itself can pose social quandaries for people when they try to use it to accomplish particular tasks. People will talk to their friends, coworkers, and families about these dilemmas, trying to figure out solutions collectively. In these moments, they are developing idioms of practice. But these are still relatively small groups deciding together how to deal with a particular problem of social etiquette. It takes time for people to develop widely agreed on strategies to use different media, especially to accomplish emotionally charged social tasks.

In the next two chapters, I discuss at greater length what people focus on as they develop their media ideologies—the structure of communicative technologies and a technology's relationship to other mediums. To understand other people's media ideologies, one has to figure out two primary aspects. First, what structures of that particular medium matter for people, and when do those structures matter? People aren't going to care all that much if a cell phone has bad reception when they are making small talk. But bad reception can become much more significant when it is happening during a breakup conversation. When ending a relationship, calling on a cell phone can become interpreted as a sign of disrespect because of the static. In other contexts, a cell phone call would be perfectly acceptable.

Second, people understand a particular medium only in the context of other media. People's media ideologies about e-mail, for example, change if they begin to text others regularly. When people start using a new technology, they change their understandings of all the other technologies they use as well. One cannot understand people's media ideology for one medium in isolation. One has to take into account their media ideologies for all the media they use, and analyze how these media ideologies are interwoven.

2

E-mail My Heart

THE STRUCTURE OF TECHNOLOGY
AND HEARTACHE

When people tell breakup stories, the structure of the technology is an integral, if often implicit, part of the story. In this chapter, I argue that the structure of the technology is profoundly social, and socially embedded in everyone's experiences. For example, technologies are often designed with particular types of users in mind—when you are not the user the designer had in mind, you can become frustrated because the piece of technology seems to resist you. To think about technology as something that is used in social interactions, but isn't social itself, would be to create a false dichotomy between people and technology, between social interactions and the equipment people use to be social. We shouldn't overlook how important people's media ideologies are in shaping how they use technology. There are many structural aspects of any medium that people could focus on when using the medium, such as the 160 character limit on a text message. People's media ideologies determine what specific aspect of how a medium affects communication will matter when they use the medium, which in turn affects how people communicate through that medium. In this chapter, I explore how technology is social, and in particular, how people's media ideologies along with the material form of the technology structure the ways people will use the medium to interact. To illustrate this, I use two breakup stories, both told to me by friends in their mid-thirties and approximately fifteen years older than most of the undergraduates I talk about in this book.[1]

The first story was told in my local yarn shop. Several women were sitting around a table covered with scattered chocolate, yarn, books, and knitting needles. I mentioned my research, and Anne laughed, announcing that she had a fabulous breakup story from long ago. She was going to the prom with a boy, he had asked her a week or two earlier. She wanted to let him know what color her prom dress was going to be so that he could choose the right corsage. Not realizing that he might have changed his mind about their prom date, she called his house. His mother answered the phone, and when Anne blithely told her the color of the dress, his mother said, "Dear, I think he is taking someone else to the prom." This is how Anne found out—his mother told her over the phone. As she laughed about the story and the stupidity of it all, I was struck by how this story depended on the fact that at that time, people only had landlines. Now that many high school students have cell phones, it is much less likely that the boyfriend's mother would answer the phone and be able to break off the relationship on behalf of the boyfriend. This breakup was doubly mediated—by the mother and the phone—but only because cell phones hadn't been invented yet.

Another friend of mine told a story in which the structure of e-mail played a significant role in the breakup. My friend, Peter, was dating someone for a few months when he gradually began to realize it wasn't working out. He told a good friend of his, Levi, that

---

1. These were stories told to me spontaneously when I started talking about my new project, so I had no handy digital recorder ready to tape their accounts.

they were probably going to break up soon, but hadn't quite gotten around to it when he and his girlfriend started talking about going to brunch with Levi. So Peter sent Levi an e-mail, explaining that he knew it might be awkward, but he would really appreciate it if Levi would have brunch with the two of them despite knowing that a breakup was imminent. Levi agreed, and they started e-mailing back and forth about where and when they would meet. Each e-mail, because of the way that e-mail is structured, contained all the previous e-mail responses. Neither Peter nor Levi could be bothered to delete the trail of replies. Finally, when it was all decided, Peter forwarded the entire e-mail trail to his then-girlfriend. Right after pressing "send," he realized that at the bottom of the e-mail was his admission that Levi already knew that he was planning to break up with his girlfriend. Horrified, he rushed over to her apartment, only to discover that she was out at a concert. He waited for her to come home so that he could end the relationship face to face instead of having her discover it accidentally at the end of an e-mail. But this would not have happened if he had been using instant messaging or texting his friend—only e-mail allows for this trail of replies.

In the introduction, I talked about how people's media ideologies revolve in part around nostalgia—they see new communicative technologies as fundamentally changing the ways that people interact. This is a common claim whenever any new technology has been introduced. When the telephone and the telegraph were new, people insisted that these inventions fundamentally changed social relationships (see Gitelman 1999 and Marvin 1988). Of course, how people experience new media as new nowadays is different than when the telephone was introduced. One of the ways in which people are experiencing these media as *new* media during breakups is that they now have so many more media through which to break up. When someone chooses to text break up, they are also choosing not to write a letter, call, or e-mail. These choices are informed by their media ideologies—how they understand what one should use a particular medium to accomplish, and how they think the medium affects the message.

The Structure of a Medium

When people would discuss their media ideologies with me, they invariably talked about the structure of the technologies as well. The way they understood how a medium influenced meaning had a lot to do with the ways they understood the medium to shape communication—the limitations and possibilities that were part of the material forms of the medium; for example, how different cell phones allowed people to text, how Facebook's interface shapes the ways people indicate a relationship is over, and so on. When people would talk about how a technology was structured, they would talk about a range of technological attributes a particular medium had. They talked about how a cell phone might get bad reception in certain places, and so using a cell phone for an important message could be a problem. Or they might describe how the Facebook news feed alerts everyone in a person's Facebook network to the breakup at the same time as it alerts the person who is being dumped. They pay attention to the second-order information that comes along with the message— whether a message is always stamped with a time and date. They also pay attention to whether second-order information can be concealed, especially whether the medium can disguise the author of the message. The structure of the medium can determine how easy it is for someone to send a message pretending to be someone else.

People also paid attention to how different media structured conversations—whether certain media allowed people to reply easily and casually to each other or not. One of the reasons some people did not like e-mail had nothing to do with formality. E-mail did not seem to encourage a rapid give-and-take.

> *Ilana:* So why are you surprised by the [idea of an] e-mail breakup?
>
> *Doyle:* I don't know, it is so settled. It is the same thing like writing a letter, this is already done, it is this big long thing. You didn't even get a chance to say anything, here it all is.

For Doyle, e-mail creates a sense of a monologue. In the abstract (Doyle had never himself experienced a mediated breakup), he would prefer electronic media that allowed for rapid turn-taking, in which people might be able to interrupt, ask questions quickly, and direct questions toward each other. For similar reasons, people often prefer instant messaging to texting as a breakup medium. Instant messaging gives a sense of simultaneous conversation. With texting, people would tell me that you would never know when someone would text you back. Someone could stop texting for a while, and you might never know the reason. Other people preferred texting because the technology seemed to enable you time to compose your reply. You could think and edit before you send the text. They liked texting precisely because it seemed less like an in-person conversation. With instant messaging, your reply appeared on their screen while you were typing. In short, one of the major concerns people had when discussing the structures of different media was how much the medium structured communication to allow for rapid conversational turn-taking, and thus to resemble in-person conversations, for better or for worse.

Not everyone cares about the same structural aspects of a medium. For some people, a cell phone's limited memory capacity made fights using a cell phone more complicated. Text fights can involve a lot of back and forth messages—halfway through a fight, you might have to clear out your inbox. Rose told me that when she is in the middle of a text-message fight, she occasionally runs into this problem:

> *Ilana:* So when do text-message fights get erased? Have you ever chosen to erase a text-message fight?
>
> *Rose:* Sometimes I have to. My inbox only holds 160 messages, and I will get through that in the middle of a fight so that it is full. You have to erase them all so that you can continue the fight. Then you have no choice. Or usually after we make up I erase them so I don't look back and get angry again....And if see a message "inbox full" then [you think], "Oh my god, what if he sent me a message, I have to delete my inbox." So that you can get a message back and start it all over again. You can have a lot of messages when you are text-message fighting, sometimes close to 200.

This is important for Rose because she and her friends will show each other carefully selected bits of their text-message fights with their boyfriends. When all of a sudden she has to erase every message in her inbox, she no longer has evidence for her friends. But what is important to Rose when she fights with someone by texting is not necessarily important to other people. Not everyone anticipates showing their friends the text messages later. For other people, the fact that you can send only short messages by text affects the text-message fight far more than the cell phone's memory capacity. In short, while most people pay attention to how certain media are materially structured, they don't focus on the same aspects of how a technology is structured. Some people focus on the fact that you need a password to read e-mail. Others ignore this aspect of e-mail and focus instead on the ability to send e-mail to many people at once. What people care about when they use Facebook or instant messaging will depend on their media ideologies as well as their communicative practices. In this chapter, I discuss how the structures of different media interact with people's media ideologies as well as their experiences of breaking up.

Since the German philosopher Martin Heidegger wrote his famous essay "The Question Concerning Technology" in 1954, scholars have engaged with the question of how and when people are aware of the structure of technology. Heidegger argues that there is a moment when a tool comes to seem like an extension of your body. At first, when you are learning to use a piece of technology, you are very aware that you and the tool are not one—you concentrate on how best to manipulate the object and it often feels awkward and unfamiliar. As you use the tool more and more, it comes to feel like a simple extension of yourself. The more it feels like an extension, the less you consciously think of how it is structured. Once you are comfortable with the technology, you become aware of its structure again only when it breaks down. When you try to use a hammer, and the head flies off and breaks a window, then you become aware again of the hammer as an object. In my interviews, however, while people might feel more or less comfortable with a medium, its structure was often crucial to the way they understood that technology as a medium of communication. Perhaps because people have so many options for communicating similar messages, the structure of a communicative technology does not always seem to fade into the background as much as Heidegger suggested.

Many of the people I interviewed had been using the various media for long enough that they didn't talk a lot about how awkward the technology was to use; for most, using the technology had become comfortable for them. Yet some people told me that they weren't fast texters and still felt a bit clumsy when texting. Though texting still didn't feel completely natural for everyone I spoke to, most were comfortable enough that they no longer had to think about where the "a" was on their phone; it was no longer hunt-and-peck texting.

This wasn't true for everyone I interviewed. One man in his fifties was learning how to text for the first time because a woman he was starting to date liked to text a lot. During their first in-person conversation, she asked Herb whether he texted or not. He told her that he didn't, but as they started seeing each other, he began to. He described to me in detail what it felt like to have to figure out how to text, how much he had to figure out and constantly think about as he texted.

Ilana: So when do you decide to text versus calling?

Herb: Usually when this woman that I am seeing texts like fun things. She has a pretty high-powered job, and so I really don't want to call her except after five or so. But I can text her anytime, and usually she texts me back. She can do it even when she is in a meeting. She can text "whassup?" the same stupid things that the kids do, little questions—"so what are your plans for tonight?" things like that. I feel like I have probably gotten twenty texts in my life, and probably most of them are from her. My kids now are starting to text [me].

Ilana: So actually texting is coming in with this relationship for you.

Herb: Yes, exactly. We have e-mail, and then phone, and now text....It was interesting because when we first met, she asked me if I texted, and I said no. I am not a text man. It was fine with her. And then I got a new phone, and I got a new contract and stuff, so I tried....And when she is driving with people in the car, who are actually driving, she can do that and have a private conversation with me. It's fun to hear a little beep and stuff....I have to really concentrate on what I am doing....

Ilana: Are you getting a texting voice?

Herb: Not that I am aware of. The woman I am texting with, she eschews a lot of abbreviations. She writes things out, and she likes that. So I am doing a lot of the same thing, I am mirroring her. But I can imagine that I will start using the numeral *4* for *for* and stuff like that, the *U* for *y-o-u*. But I don't think I have a texting voice. Sometimes I can't get a capital, I have to keep figuring out how to get that. It always starts with a capital, but then when I do the second time, it doesn't work. And sometimes I have all capitals. It is too early to tell.

Ilana: I am very curious about the moment in which people are picking up new technologies. And what are the moments where you have to figure out how all this technology is working. So the capital letter is one of them.

Herb: And all the punctuation. Basically there is a menu thing.

Ilana: So are you an apostrophe man? Do you use apostrophes in texting?

Herb: Yes, I think I am still mirroring the other person. But I can see with the efficiency thing that you can just drop that out.

Herb talks about all the new decisions he has to make in learning how to text. He not only has to figure out the mechanics of texting such as where certain symbols are. He also has to decide what his texting style is going to be—does he use apostrophes or not? Does he shorten words or spell them out? He talks about this in terms of his new relationship; he was learning to text with a particular audience in mind. Using a piece of technology is never entirely transparent; people always have to learn how to use it. They are also always learning in social contexts; the learning itself is a reflection on the relationships underlying any communication. In addition, when people are using technology, they are making social choices, like how formally to write their texts. They are also making decisions about how to communicate that will have social consequences for the ways people respond to their messages.

Learning to Use a Medium

Because I am interested in how people learn to use technologies, for the rest of the chapter I will focus on Facebook—the medium college students most often talked to me about learning how to use. People are not just learning how to manipulate an object when they learn to use a particular medium. They are also always learning what the social expectations might be about communicating through a particular medium. One has to learn how to read a Facebook profile, for example. Some people, mostly women, will link their relationship status to a friends' profile, although the relationship is strictly platonic. The typical link is between a straight woman and a straight female friend, but I have also interviewed other permutations: straight women linked to their female cousins, straight women who are linked to gay men, straight men who link to other straight men, and straight men who link to platonic straight female friends. In all these cases, it was clear in my interviews that nothing romantic was going on between the people linked. But people viewing these profiles have to learn to read the profiles to interpret whether the relationship status is a serious claim or not. One woman explained to me that before she arrived on campus, she thought her resident assistant (RA) was a lesbian because she was engaged to a woman on Facebook. Once she arrived, she quickly realized that this was not the case; she learned that her RA had a boyfriend and was choosing not to reveal this on Facebook. One's relationship status may seem reasonably straightforward when one first fills out the profile information (although perhaps not if one is tempted to put "it's complicated" as the relationship status). However the way people actually use the status category makes it far from transparent. People have to spend some time learning to interpret the different ways that those in their Facebook networks will use this category—a type of education necessary for all communicative technologies.

People have to learn the social uses of technology not only because the people around them are using these technologies in specific and often learnable ways but also because the technologies themselves will presume certain social narratives. Technologies ensure that people interact with them in particular ways; that is, the technologies presuppose certain kinds of social relationships. The relationship status on Facebook is an apt example of the kinds of social relations that technologies presuppose. For those readers not familiar with the Facebook of 2010, a user can choose whether or not to have their relationship status visible on their profile. If they decide they want their relationship status announced, they have to choose one of seven options from the drop-down menu: single, in a relationship, engaged, married, it's complicated, in an open relationship, or widowed.[2] For every category except "single" or "widowed," the user can then provide a name—"in a relationship with *Frodo Baggins*" or "it's complicated with *Johnny Depp.*" If Frodo Baggins or Johnny Depp don't have a Facebook profile, or don't confirm the relationship request, then the profile will only list the fact that the person is in a relationship (or it's complicated), not with whom the person is in a relationship. There are many ways in which this category presupposes certain kinds of social

2. Widowed was an option added August 2009, and was not an option when I conducted my interviews.

interactions and prevents others. For example, there is a presupposition of monogamy, even in the category "in an open relationship." After all, a user can only be in an open relationship with one other person. This is something I noticed about the relationship status categories, but whenever I mention it in class or in my interviews, people express surprise. They often take monogamy for granted to such an extent that they don't notice that even the open relationship category assumes monogamy in how the category allows people to link their profile to others' profiles.

In short, technology always condenses historical and social assumptions about how people interact. Users might readily adopt or agree with some of these assumptions. For example, the designers of Facebook clearly thought that it might be important to indicate on one's profile not only whether one is a relationship but what kind of relationship one is in (open, complicated, engaged). As I discuss later in this chapter, many people agree that this is crucial information.

Imagining Designers, Imagining Users

Designers' social insights into those people who might be the likely users are not always accurate. For example, in 2007, Facebook offers people the opportunity to add the honesty box application to their profile. The honesty box enables one's Facebook friends to write messages anonymously to the profile. If the writer wishes, they can allow gender to be visible (messages from self-defined men are blue, messages from self-defined women are pink). Other than gender, there is no identifying mark on the message, unless the writer chooses to reveal their identity in the text of the message. When I asked some interviewees if they had the honesty box, they would respond: "what's that?" When I explained, they would react in horror, wondering why anyone would put that on their profile at all. Janine responded in a fairly typical fashion for people who thought the honesty box was a bad idea: "You can be anonymous and you can tell people what you like think, but what's the point of that? You're just going to probably hurt their feelings and they're not going to even know you said it, so what's the point? I mean, if you actually wanted to say this to somebody like that to be mean, but don't say it to their face or something like that, what's the point?" People quickly imagined that others would write critical and undermining statements to a person's profile without any of the consequences of being known as the author. The social possibilities the honesty box might create made the idea of the honesty box a poor choice indeed for these interviewees. While Facebook's description of the honesty box indicates that its designers imagined that the honesty box might give people the chance to reveal secret crushes (which presumably is a positive), my interviewees who responded negatively to the honesty box didn't think of secret crushes at all, only of insults.[3]

The people I interviewed were well aware that technologies were designed, and thus could be designed in other ways. In part, this is because technologies had been changing so rapidly for people. People could remember owning cell phones that didn't allow them to have ringtones[4] or to take photos. Facebook has changed rapidly since people first began using it—from the news feed to numerous applications. When I talked to people about how they were using Facebook, they often commented on the fact that someone had

---

3. Not everyone reacted in horror to the honesty box; some did find it appealing. Even so, people who told me about using the honesty box did not often mention finding out about secret crushes or insults.

4. Ringtones are melodies or sounds that announce a phone call on a cell phone.

designed the interface, and talked about these features as changeable. When I asked Elizabeth what she thought "it's complicated" as a Facebook relationship status was used for, she started wondering who had even decided to add that option to the possible categories, imagining the business meetings in which this might have taken place.

> "It's complicated" and "open relationship"…you have to think about it from all angles, since obviously some people do use it. It's just weird how people come up with it and are like "people are going to want to be in an open relationship" or "it's complicated." That's what I think is really interesting—the people who decided what is important enough to be on Facebook.…I would like to be involved in that.

While Elizabeth was the only one who imagined in detail the meeting in which this decision might be made, others expressed the belief that the designers did not have them in mind when they created certain features. Halle told me how emotionally difficult it was to cancel a relationship on Facebook by clicking on the "cancel" button because, as I mentioned earlier, the Facebook software always double checks if someone is canceling a relationship on purpose when they change their relationship status. Halle told me that she and her friend had written a message to Facebook, requesting that Facebook send a reassuring message after compelling someone to press "confirm."

> *Ilana:* What did you do about your relationship status on Facebook?
>
> *Halle:* It said we were in a relationship.…Yeah, I broke up with him, but it's still devastating after three years. It's just another thing you have to do, and click "cancel" on a relationship. I mean, c'mon! So we [Halle and her best friend] wrote a little note to

> Facebook where you could write comments, saying: "We think you should send people who cancel their relationships on Facebook a note saying 'Don't worry, there's other fishes in the sea.'"

Halle and others recognized that technologies had social expectations that some designer had built into the software or the structure of the communication device. These were expectations that could be transformed to accommodate their own social requirements if they could figure out the right avenues for convincing the designers to change the software.

One man I interviewed, Yi-Lun, strongly objected to using the relationship status category because it was designed and also seemed to presume that certain social narratives were at play. He explained that he didn't like the idea of having his unpredictable relationships defined in the terms that some nameless software programmer had predetermined. As he put it,

> Defining a relationship with a drop-down menu takes a lot of mystery out of a new relationship. I don't mind doing it, but it is more like I just don't feel like I am making a decision when I do it. Or I don't feel like I am in control of my own relationship. Because it is like I have to do this just because Facebook has it as an option. Just because some programmer made it an option, now it's become a part of my life—it defines my relationships.

When people are using communication technologies to break up with each other, they are not only navigating their social relationships but also dealing with the ways these technologies seem to structure social interactions. These technologies are social, just like the people using them. Just as the people believe social interactions should unfold in particular ways, so the technologies contain embedded narratives about how interactions should take place. These technologies are not outside of the social, determining social interaction. They are designed and distributed by people with assumptions about how social relationships should take place. Thus when people are using these technologies to break up with each other, they are not just having a breakup conversation with their romantic partner; they are also in dialogue with the embedded social narratives of the communicative technologies they are using. To explain this with a concrete example, let's turn to some stories I collected about how people dealt with the social narratives embedded in Facebook's relationship status category as they were beginning and ending romantic relationships with other people. In turning to the Facebook relationship status, I will be addressing how the structures of these new technologies are affecting the ways in which people are disconnecting.

Facebook Official

Because of Facebook's news feed, when you announce that you are in a relationship on Facebook, you are announcing this fact to everyone able to see your Facebook profile. This also means that you are opening up the possibility that at some point you may be announcing that you have broken up with someone as well. Thus making a relationship "Facebook official" has certain social consequences, not the least of which involves dealing with making a possible future breakup Facebook official and thus public as well. I want to stress that the news feed has significantly affected the consequences of making a breakup official on Facebook. Before the news feed, people had to click on a particular profile to find out whether or not that person was still in a relationship. Because this took some effort, upon learning about a friend's breakup through Facebook, people were faced with the question of whether they openly admit to that friend or acquaintance that they had noticed the announced ending of that relationship on Facebook. Before the news feed, to know about a relationship via Facebook was to admit to a curiosity that could easily be interpreted as unseemly. Everyone might know about the breakup, but not everyone was willing to act on this knowledge. After the news feed, everyone in your network knows about the Facebook breakup whether or not they have clicked on your profile. As Amelie put it, the news feed is there for people who are nosy, but lazy. The news feed also guarantees that if you announce the beginning or ending of your relationship on Facebook, you are effectively telling everyone in your Facebook network that you are with someone or have broken up.

Because of the public nature of this announcement, people have to strategize about making a relationship Facebook official. For some people, a relationship is not a relationship until it is Facebook official—and there can be an intermediate stage in a relationship now, officially unofficial. Alice told me that friends of hers were at this stage, in part because her female friend did not want to let her ex-boyfriend know that she was seeing someone new.

> *Alice:* And then she's actually been dating another guy since then, but they're like officially unofficial. It's like we all know that they're boyfriend and girlfriend. But one of the things she's talking about, like, whether or not they were Facebook official yet. And it just seemed bizarre to me, I'm like "Is that really a question at this point?" They have not yet made the decision because to them that means official if you're, if you're officially in a relationship, then your Facebook says, "In a relationship with...."
>
> *Ilana:* Have they had a relationship conversation yet?
>
> *Alice:* Yeah, they talk about it all the time. She's not sure she wants to be...She is in a relationship with him, but is she sure she wants to call it that? Because of her ex-boyfriend, and so it's not posted on Facebook.

Ilana: When do you think she is going to make it official?

Alice: I don't know, I think she caught herself calling him her boyfriend the other day, and she's like "Wait, he is my boyfriend, isn't he?" We're like, "Yeah, he sure is." It's like "Why don't I call him that?" And always, like "No." It's like almost a thing where she knows she's being weird about it, but she can't, she doesn't feel that she can stop being weird. And so until she decides it's going to be OK, if she like says it out loud, "OK, he's my boyfriend, we're in a relationship, I'm no longer with my ex, that's different then…" I guess until then they literally call it officially unofficial. That is what she told me.

This intermediate stage does not seem to substantially change Alice's friends' behavior as a couple; they are constantly in each other's company and noticeably a couple in their dorm life. But they are not performing their relationship on Facebook, and thus not necessarily informing their friends who do not live in their dorm.

Facebook's relationship status thus presents people with a social dilemma—whether to use this medium to circulate information about togetherness. Some people view this as an inappropriate way to let their friends know of important changes and will wait a week or two before changing their relationship status on Facebook. This applied to becoming a couple, engagements as well as breakups. Lydia told me:

I got engaged this summer, and we waited for three or four weeks before we put it on Facebook because we wanted to make sure everyone we knew really well found out from us. It seemed like a "happy birthday" because when we put "engaged with," there was a flood. "You got engaged, oh my god!" "You are engaged!" People will try to contact everyone they are close to first, and tell them personally.

While some people eschew using Facebook as the vehicle for announcing a breakup to their close friends, other people see this as preferable. One person I interviewed talked about how a couple he knew posted a notice on Facebook explaining the breakup.

> *Paul:* I had two friends, they were going out since August of '06. And they went out, and it was the summer before he goes off to college. And she goes to a community college. So they didn't know what to do, so they decided to stay together. He went to University of San Francisco; it was a seven-hour trip, so it was kind of far away. So whenever they talked, they always argued, always fighting. They are talking by cell phones. I am better friends with one person [the woman], and she and cell phones don't mix together. So I always sent her Facebook messages or something. Everyone knew it was on the rocks. And then he went home for fall break, and they ended it there. We're not going to go out, but we are not going to see other people. We are just going to see.

> *Ilana:* That's weird.

> *Paul:* Yeah, it was like "we are going to be friends, maybe this break will help us."

> *Ilana:* Oh, so they are taking a break, they are not breaking up.

> *Paul:* Yeah, that's it. But on Facebook, she put single, so we all knew something happened. And then the next day I got a page-long Facebook message from her. This is her and him writing this together, and they explain the whole situation—why they broke up. And they thanked everyone for trying to help them out. And I think that they wrote that so they wouldn't have to explain to every single person why they broke up. But I think people are starting to use Facebook as their means for telling people *why* they broke up, how they broke up, and the reasons they did break up. I think it's just an easier mode of communication instead of calling on the phone or talking to people in person. And everyone is away at college.

> *Ilana:* So you get this note—what do you do with a note like that?

> *Paul:* I get this note, I am just reading it. Nothing was shocking me, because I know these people. It was like "yeah, yeah, yeah."

So I wrote back "thanks for the notice." Not "message," "thanks for the *notice.*"

Paul explained that he found this an unusual way to announce a breakup, and wondered if this was now going to be a standard way that people used Facebook. He even responded to the Facebook message in a way that expressed that he found this a bit odd. In a sense, this was a couple who did the reverse of waiting to post an engagement or breakup online until they contact everyone they are close to. Instead, Facebook became the medium of choice for the couple to circulate not only the fact of the breakup but also the reasons they wanted publicly understood.

Given that posting one's relationship status on Facebook is such a public act, there are a variety of reasons why people would not want to do so. Some people are anticipating breaking up with the person they are in a relationship with. For example, Kelsey told me about refusing to be Facebook official while she was a senior in high school because she did not want a long-distance relationship in college.

Ilana: So were you in a relationship on Facebook too?

Kelsey: I never really changed it to "I'm in a relationship." It was a weird relationship....I just left it on single....I didn't really want to put it up and then when we broke up, having to take it down. All those questions coming at me. Versus if I just left it as it was, people would ask me. Actually people would ask me *a lot,* like every week, "Did you break up with him? Did you break up with him?" They would ask me the next week, and the next week. Maybe I should have just put it up on Facebook.

Kelsey knew, as many others told me, that if she posted her relationship status on Facebook, she would be barraged with questions about the breakup. But this strategy backfired for her a bit.

All of her friends thought that she should break up. So when her relationship status remained blank on her profile, they had to ask her directly. She got tired of being asked every week or so whether she had broken up yet or not, but she also recognized that this constant questioning was the price of not announcing her relationship status on Facebook.

Not everyone sees the decision to put their relationship status on Facebook as a comment on how committed they are to their current lover. Some are in networks where this is simply not done. Some don't quite understand what is happening in their relationship, and so are reluctant to discuss it publicly. Yet others consider it no one else's business. Several people told me that if someone else was genuinely interested, they could always ask the person directly. Some find the social emphasis on Facebook disconcerting and don't want to contribute to the social dramas created by posting their status. All these reasons have to be negotiated when the person begins to date someone who does want to announce the relationship via Facebook.

Katie's story illustrates this dilemma. Katie was not comfortable with Facebook as a serious record of her life. To express this unease, she announced on Facebook that she was "in a relationship" with her friend's dog, who had its own Facebook profile. Then she started dating Dirk.

> *Katie:* It was a long-distance relationship. And when it started out, everything was fine except that he was upset with me because on my Facebook, I put I was in a relationship with my friend's dog on Facebook. So it was just a big joke, and I wasn't going to take it down because it's Facebook. I don't think it's really a big deal. I don't need that to verify a relationship.
>
> *Ilana:* And think of the poor dog—how can you hurt the poor dog's feelings?

Katie: I know, that's what I said. I was like: "I can't do that to him."
But he [her boyfriend] wanted me to take it down, and I didn't
for a while because of the point that he felt like I needed to pub-
licize it. Because to me it's not anybody's business who I am dating and when I start dating them and when it stops. But for him,
it was like we're not really in a relationship until we put that up.

Katie eventually changed her relationship status to please her boyfriend. For Katie, her new boyfriend's concern with Facebook was
a bit baffling. She didn't value the Facebook relationship status as a
public assertion of commitment as he did. For her, the decisions
people made outside of Facebook seemed as valid and consequen-
tial as those they portrayed themselves to have made on Facebook.
This difference in perspective became especially apparent when
they broke up after a few months. She ended the relationship with
him through Skype, an Internet-based way to call people through
computers (since they were in a long-distance relationship, this
was the cheapest way for them to communicate).

We broke up that night, and it was really late. It was probably 12:30
or 1 Eastern time, and it was 6:30 a.m. for him. It's kind of weird,
I was literally lying in bed and waited until it was at least 6 to call
him. At that point, for me it was over. And even people at work
knew the next day, because some of my friends knew that we were
having a lot of problems. I was thinking of breaking up with him,
and they knew the next day. I had told them that we broke up last
night. So for me, that's when it's official, whenever I go and tell
that person "we're breaking up." We are broken up now. And then
we talked on Skype the next day....He wanted me to explain stuff
more, and so I did. That was fine. And after that, I thought that was
enough explanation. But apparently once I took my status down
as being in a relationship with him [a few days later]—I didn't
change it to single, I didn't change it to being in a relationship with
someone else, I just took it [the "relationship status" category] off

completely. He sent me a message on Facebook saying: "I guess its official now because you took it off your profile." I actually sent him a message back that said "Wasn't it official whenever we broke up over the phone?"

For Dirk, the Facebook relationship status was an indicator of how serious Katie was about ending the relationship. Katie had a different understanding about what it might mean to end the relationship on Facebook. For her, the relationship was over as soon as they had the breakup conversation. For Dirk, it wasn't definitively over until she changed her Facebook relationship status.

Because Facebook's relationship status is both so public and so symbolically loaded, people have different ways of including it in their breakup. Keith talked about how he and his ex-girlfriend changed their relationship status together, partially as a ritual way to signal to each other that the breakup was a friendly one.

> We broke up for a while, for a week, maybe two weeks. We wanted to let it settle in. I knew what was going to happen. But we wanted to let it settle in for a while with each other until we made it this big public ordeal, outside of the people that already knew. It was about a week or two weeks later, she had come over to my house and we were talking. And I said, "I think we should take this down [i.e., the "in a relationship" status on their profiles]." So we did it together, we didn't put "single" up or anything like that. We just took it off completely. So it wasn't like a big deal, and we did it together so one person didn't seem to be saying: "F— you, I am single now." Because it wasn't like that so much.

Keith was aware, as were others I talked to, that changing one's relationship status on Facebook has repercussions. Others in their Facebook networks might contact them, perhaps to ask why the breakup happened. Given how friendly Keith and his girlfriend's breakup was, it was possible for them to anticipate and plan for when they were willing to deal with the repercussions of no longer being Facebook official.

Keith's story was unusual; I did not hear any other stories about a couple deciding to end their relationship on Facebook while they were hanging out together. More commonly, I heard stories of people changing their relationship status from "in a relationship" to "it's complicated" and then to "single" as a way to signal their unhappiness and anger to their girlfriend or boyfriend. In these cases, it was a public performance—everyone in their networks found out about this through the news feed. But it was a public message with primarily one person in mind as the target audience—one's lover. These public exchanges allowed everyone else to know that the relationship was in trouble for a week or two before the actual breakup. Thus breaking up could involve an online audience, when, prior to Facebook, one would have to have loud fights at parties to make a similar public statement.

Having a Facebook official relationship sometimes changed the ways in which the relationship dissolved. Yi-Lun explained to me that most of his relationships in the past had ended because of his traveling. He would be in a part of the United States for a short period of time, and the relationship would slowly dissolve after both people had moved away. But because he was sometimes in a relationship on Facebook, this required an explicit negotiation that he would have preferred not to have.

> *Yi-Lun:* We were still together when she left. But then it was kind of weird, it was like we kept talking, we were Skyping because I was going over on my cell phone minutes, and talking on Facebook....I think we stayed together on Facebook for maybe a month. But after that, after a couple of weeks, I think we made a deadline. So we said: "Alright, what do we do with Facebook?"

"I don't know, I don't know, let's talk about it in a week." So we just kind of put it off. And then we were like, "alright, what do we do about this?" And then we decided, "alright, in two weeks, let's take it off." And then in two weeks we just took it off. It was a mutual thing. And we kept talking. And I didn't put back up single or anything. I guess that's the way my relationships have been because I tend to travel. When I was in Taiwan, I was with a girl. And then when I left, we just kind of fizzled.

Ilana: And the problem with making something Facebook official...

Yi-Lun: Is that it's still there. So the fizzling isn't possible. You have to make a conscious decision to do that. I don't know what it would have been like if I had said "so what do we do about this Facebook?" And she said, "I say we still keep it until things are absolutely sure that we are not going to get back together." If she wasn't as understanding about that or if I wasn't, then it would have been like "c'mon, what are we doing here?" But I think we both had an understanding of what was going on.

One of Yi-Lun's objections to being Facebook official is that what might have been a gentle dissolution to a relationship had to be far more explicit because of Facebook's relationship status.

Because of the structure of the technology, when people change their relationship status, they also have to decide what they are changing the status *to*. People talked about handling this in three different ways. Some people took the status off entirely, and spent a week or even several months without any indication on their profile of whether they were single or involved with anyone. They would not add their relationship status to their profile again until they were in a relationship that required being Facebook official again, for whatever reason. Sometimes people changed their status to "single." Occasionally people, primarily women, took advantage of the way the relationship status was structured to link their profiles to a good friend in the aftermath of a breakup. Kathleen explained: "Its amazing the people who come out of the woodwork when you end a relationship on Facebook. It is completely bizarre. And of course right after [the breakup] I "married" my best girlfriend on Facebook to say "I don't *need* you at all." In these instances, ending the relationship on Facebook was too difficult without publicly announcing that there were others who still cared about you, that you might no longer be romantically involved with someone, but you were not alone.

Implied Users, Actual Users

As people described what they did with the Facebook relationship status category, it sometimes became apparent that the user the designer had imagined was not the user I was talking to. There could be quite a gap between the *implied user* of a piece of technology—that is, who the designer thought might use the piece of technology as they designed it—and the *actual user,* the person I was interviewing about their uses of the technology.[5] This sometimes became apparent in the most unexpected moments as people were figuring out how they wanted to use the Facebook relationship category during a breakup. In class, one student explained how he changed the relationship status to single in the aftermath of a breakup. A day later, he decided that this was ridiculous; he didn't want any statement about his romantic life on his Facebook profile. He removed his relationship status entirely, and so his news feed announced, "Henry is no longer single." This wasn't true—he just no longer wanted the world to

5. Madeline Akrich (1992) inspired my discussion of implied user versus actual user and the social narratives embedded in technology.

know about his relationship status. Yet in trying to remove his status, he managed to remind everyone in his news feed of his status and perhaps give them the impression he was in a relationship. Facebook's interface continued to signal exactly what he had decided no longer to let people know, and worse, did so through the news feed. Moments like these reveal to people that they are not the users that the designers of the technology presumed they would be.

When people talk about the ways in which the structure of the relationship status category affects their interactions, they also mention the consequences of trying to avoid dealing with the relationship status. Gwen told me that she deactivated her Facebook profile rather than have to deal with friends' responses to the news feed announcement that she had broken up. "One of the reasons I went through with deleting Facebook is because I didn't want my relationship status to change from being 'in a relationship with so-and-so' to 'single.'" Deactivating allowed her to avoid the inevitable Facebook messages and phone calls that can accompany a Facebook announcement of a breakup. Indeed, some women told me they fielded phone calls for three to seven days after they announced the breakup on Facebook. This is one of the consequences people are beginning to anticipate whenever they change their relationship status—they will have to spend a few days explaining the story of the breakup to people. When Gwen decided to deactivate her account, she was trying to avoid this consequence. She didn't even tell anyone she was going to do this. But deactivating her account without letting anyone know that she had done so had its own repercussions. For her, the deactivation was directly linked to the breakup, she simply didn't want to change her relationship status. Friends of hers, however, noticed that she was no longer in their list of friends and were concerned that she was angry at them. No one asked her about this directly, but some of her friends asked others why Gwen had decided to defriend them. Even the solutions people imaginatively create to address the social dilemmas technological structures can pose can, in turn, generate more social complications.

The relationship status category on Facebook has affected people's breakups in a number of ways. First, breakups have the potential to be public in a new way. Announcing one's breakup on Facebook is a different way of circulating information than the ways people used to gossip before. This information circulates, not because someone has actively told someone else, but because people simply log in to Facebook. People can know about friends' love lives even though they haven't spoken to that friend in months, or even spoken to anyone who has spoken to that friend in months. This is not a dramatic change in the way people circulate social information. In the past, many groups of college friends had one or two members who always seemed to know what was going on with everyone else and let everyone else know whether a breakup had happened. When I was discussing this point with my class, I remarked, "These people are now out of a social job." But my students quickly corrected me: These individuals might not announce the breakup anymore, but they are the ones who know why the breakup has happened. So their job has changed a little— they no longer announce the breakup, they announce the reasons for the breakup.

Second, I may be noticing that the relationship status affects people's romances because I was interviewing on a U.S. college campus. On the I.U. campus so many people are involved with Facebook that anyone in a relationship has to decide whether to be Facebook official. Yet I have some indication that this concern with being Facebook official is becoming more widespread. Amelie told me the following about her boss, whom Amelie thought was around thirty:

> She [her boss] met him on eHarmony.[6] She did meet him in person a couple of times, but they have mostly had a long-distance relationship because he lives in New York, and she lives in Trenton, New Jersey. [S]he told me that she didn't feel comfortable with the fact that it was a relationship until her Facebook status was changed. She literally was questioning whether they were actually dating until it was official on Facebook. As soon as that happens, she goes, "okay, its official, we're dating, we're together, we are a couple."

As Amelie's story shows, even for people who never were on Facebook in college, being Facebook official has now become a widespread expectation. One cannot simply forget to put one's relationship status on Facebook—this is always a conscious and calculated decision. In college, people are constantly evaluating other people's relationships, so one's friends will invariably ask—are you Facebook official yet? Being Facebook official has offered a way to be explicit about one's relationship, with all the prices that such explicitness tends to bring. One has to end relationships explicitly and publicly; relationships are evaluated by others in terms of how "Facebook official" they might be; and, as Yi-Lun points out, some flexibility and ambiguity is lost along the way.

What Is New about New Media?

I have been arguing that technologies are social, that to see technological structures as separate from people's social interactions

---

6. eHarmony is a web-based dating site.

is to misunderstand how people and technology interact and how people experience new media as new. The structures of different communicative technologies are suggesting social ways of interaction and social narratives that people then have to respond to. People have to decide whether to incorporate, change, or reject these social narratives. This is a process that often seems to baffle people, if the questions I get when I talk about my research publicly are any indication. The first time I went to another campus to talk about my work, a bright undergraduate asked (I am paraphrasing), "Have you looked at how these technologies are changing the way people have relationships—not my generation, but the generation after me? Why are middle-school students having Facebook relationships? These Facebook relationships aren't real relationships." She wanted to know if such relationships would change the ways people will be intimate. I was a bit thrown by this question. First, I was surprised to hear an undergraduate say she was not in the same generation as someone a few years younger than she was. And I was puzzled that she thought these Facebook relationships weren't "real." Breaking up by Facebook, or texting, or instant messaging is very real—the breakup conversation can have the real effect of ending the romantic relationship. So why aren't relationships largely conducted through these media "real" relationships? But most important, I was also struck by the implicit assumption that technology and people are separate, that technology is somehow outside of social interactions and shaping these social interactions. Or, put another way, that technology determines social interactions, but that social interactions do not determine technology—that she considered the relationship between people and technology a one-way street.

Historians of media have argued that the assumption that technology is determinant and potentially hazardous is a common response in North America and Europe whenever any new communicative technology is introduced (see Gitelman 2006, Marvin 1988, Peters 1999, Sconce 2000). As Carolyn Marvin points out, this anxiety revolves around the idea that technology determines and transforms social interactions in unpredictable ways that undermine the more certain knowledge one appears to have by talking to someone face to face (1988, 87). She argues that new technologies such as the telephone were seen as creating risky possibilities for romance.

> New forms of communication created unprecedented opportunities not only for courting and infidelity, but also for romancing unacceptable persons outside one's own class, and even one's own race, in circumstances that went unobserved by the regular community. The potential for illicit sexual behavior had obvious and disquieting power to undermine accustomed centers of moral authority and social order. (Marvin 1988, 70)

Marvin focuses on the inappropriate and even risky romances people believe might accompany the introduction of new media. Technologies introduced the possibilities of new connections; people soon began to wonder who else could be contacted by these new means. Jeffrey Sconce writes about how people began to rethink the possibilities of communicating with the dead when the telegraph was introduced. Because this technology introduced disembodied communication across previously unimaginable distances, it also opened up the possibility that people could communicate with anyone they imagined as disembodied, and especially the dead. "Talking with the dead through raps and knocks, after all, was only slightly more miraculous than talking with the living yet absent through dots and dashes; both involved subjects reconstituted through technology as an entity at once interstitial and uncanny" (Sconce 2000, 28).

These are both relatively recent examples. Yet even in ancient Greece, people worried that new media would be altering intimate relations for the worse. John Durham Peters talks about how, in the *Phaedrus*, Socrates thought that writing was harming communication, that the move from spoken to written communication was dangerous.

> Socrates provides a checklist of enduring anxieties that arise in response to transformations in the means of communication. Writing parodies live presence; it is inhuman, lacks interiority, destroys authentic dialogue, is impersonal, and cannot acknowledge the individuality of its interlocutors; and it is promiscuous in distribution....Communication must be soul-to-soul, among embodied live people, in an intimate interaction that is uniquely fit for each participant. (Peters 1999, 47)

In short, worrying about how new communicative technologies might alter the ways people can safely form their social relationships with others is not new, nor is it peculiar to the Internet or cell phone. It is a historical pattern in North America and Europe to believe that the risk lies with the structures of these technologies and to worry that these new technologies will change the quality of relationships.

So when I hear questions like the one that the bright undergraduate asked me about whether Facebook teaches middle-school students to have unreal relationships, I worry that my answer might reinforce the idea that technology is not social or that technology can determine social interaction. At the same time, I want to be careful—I don't want to dismiss this concern out of hand just because Americans have thought something similar with every new technological innovation. The people I interviewed told me in no uncertain terms that there were ways that the structures of the technology had profoundly changed themselves and their relationships. Who am I to say dismissively, "but you Americans always think this, you always think that technology trumps and changes the social as if technology isn't social itself in the first place." The common theme in my interviews—how people are experiencing the newness of these technologies—deserves to be taken seriously. In this section, I discuss two ways that the structures of these technologies, and Facebook in particular, impact how people are having relationships.

As discussed previously, Facebook is affecting how many people have romantic relationships. Anyone who has a Facebook account has to decide whether and how to use the relationship status category. The possibility of having a "Facebook official" relationship means that people now have a way to demonstrate publicly that they have an explicit and publicly accepted relationship. "Facebook official" resembles the familiar markers of a form of dating that people haven't practiced in college for a couple of decades—no one has had such clear external signs of being involved exclusively with someone else since women stopped getting pinned or wearing their boyfriend's class ring around their neck. Anne and her mother, for example, thought that becoming "Facebook official" was the contemporary equivalent to "going steady" in her parents' generation:

> *Anne:* My dad is like, "What's Facebook? What are you talking about?" I am at dinner with them and I'll tell my mom, "Chris hasn't added me as a Facebook relationship. I don't know what to do."
>
> *And Mom'll say:* "Maybe he's not ready."
>
> *And my dad is like:* "What the hell is going on? What are you talking about? What is this Facebook"
>
> "Dad, don't worry about it. You don't even know how to text message."

And she [Anne's mother] tries to equate it to real-life things. "Now they are in a relationship on Facebook, which means what we would call going steady."

Anne's mother realizes, as does Anne, that people are using the category "Facebook official" to stand in for a public display of commitment in the relationship in ways similar to older U. S. styles of dating. Facebook official has come to stand in for exclusivity, in part because being Facebook official makes it that much harder to be involved with more than one person at a time.

Potato Chips of Information

While the structure of Facebook may be creating some nostalgic analogies such as "going steady" for people in relationships, others remarked how the structure of Facebook encouraged them to be anxious selves or to have relationships filled with jealous monitoring. Many of these new media technologies let a level of monitoring be easy and accessible that in the past used to require considerable effort and imagination. Several women told me that the ease of monitoring their boyfriend on Facebook changed them. Facebook made them into *that kind of girlfriend,* the one who is ever-suspicious and constantly asking her boyfriend to prove he only thinks of her. Olivia, an undergraduate I interviewed, explained what led her to deactivate her Facebook account:

> People always ask me, "Why did you delete Facebook?" And I want to say that it kind of led to the demise of my last relationship, as crazy as that sounds. . . . It didn't necessarily end it specifically, I had this boyfriend who I knew was a very outgoing guy. This is how we got to talking, because I can be pretty shy sometimes. He has a lot of girlfriends. The first time I met him, we walked into the

restaurant where he worked, and these girls just flocked to him, they are hugging him and all these things. And at first, I am a very trustworthy person, I trust my family and my friends, and I don't have any issues with that. So I was just blindly going, "Well, I don't blame them. He's a great guy, he's a great friend. He is very friendly, he is just as friendly with my guy friends, my family." And then as we get more serious, I start to see the pictures come up. I was not twenty-one and of drinking age, and he had just turned twenty-one and [was] at the bars. I am not gutsy enough to go out with a fake ID, and so we only went out a couple of times together. And every other picture was his face mashed up against another girl's face. And they are hugging him, and these girls, you know you can write your caption, and every girl writes, "Oh, I love Brian so much, isn't Brian so cute, isn't he awesome? You're my lover Brian!" And remember, for a long time, I was like, well you know, I have flirted with guys in this way and meant nothing by it. It is possible to have girl friends, and not to have infidelity involved. Eventually my good friends were saying, "Hey, have you looked at Brian's Facebook lately?" My friend wasn't trying to start anything, it was just as a concerned friend. How do you look at these things and be normal with that? And when it got so bad that my friends were trying to tell me—are you sure he is an okay guy? I started to really wonder. That's how it begins. At first it just became this obsession with checking his Facebook, and wondering, "Who did you go out with?" And that's how these text-message fights begin. I am at home in my apartment alone, and I ask him who he is with, and he says a girl's name. I find her on Facebook, and oh look, a string of pictures with her. And then you start looking at these girls—Is she skinnier than me? Is she prettier than me?...I would ask him what did you do this weekend? And I can go on his Facebook and I can see what his weekend looked like.

Facebook allowed Olivia to compare her boyfriend's answers with the "evidence" on Facebook. She was also very aware that he did not have his own cell phone camera. Because the pictures of him were pictures that other people put up of him, these photos served as more accidental (and thus more reliable) evidence of what he was doing. It seemed that he wasn't managing his Facebook profile, that his Facebook profile was being created for him by the traces of how friendly he was at parties. So Olivia asked, and checked, and asked and checked. She describes how she found herself becoming paranoid, discovering a side of herself that she did not want to have. Finally Olivia got so disgusted with the cycle that she quit Facebook. A few months later, she broke up with him.

Olivia was concerned largely about how she was becoming a different self, a less trusting person, when she interacted with Facebook. Other people who quit Facebook felt that it allowed people to monitor each other too much, to see too much about what their boyfriends or girlfriends did and who might be flirting with them. When people told me how detrimental the structure of Facebook was, they insisted that it was the kind of information that was available. Gwen explained why she deactivated her Facebook profile this way:

> I feel like I couldn't decide whether it was the fact that I checked Facebook that triggered my not trusting him, or I already didn't trust him, and Facebook just perpetuated it. We really didn't have issues until I started seeing things on Facebook, like photos. And then I started thinking "oh, I had better ask him about this." And then anytime something new was put up, it just got worse and worse. And most of my arguments with him about something that he did, I would not have even known about had I not been on Facebook. I would have been completely oblivious and it wasn't things that I *should* know. It just didn't matter.

While people complained to me about Facebook offering too much information about the minutiae of their boyfriends' or girlfriends' lives, I am not convinced that this is the problem. Rather, I think the problem is that Facebook allows for enough information to cause people to wonder, but not enough information to satisfy this curiosity. In this sense, Facebook offers potato chips of information—you get a tantalizing taste that somehow doesn't quite satisfy, and so you keep seeking a sensation of fulfillment, of being satiated. Facebook offers the hope of certain knowledge, but rarely does one ever fully know for certain whether or not someone is actually flirting with your lover, whether or not your lover is actually being unfaithful, and so on. This, for those readers who have wondered, may be why people can spend countless hours on Facebook. When I explained this theory to Gwen, she answered with a story:

> One time, I do have one friend who is now in Germany so she can't help me anymore, who was friends with him on Facebook. And one day, we just looked him up. We were in class, she had her laptop, and we weren't listening. And she said, "Let's look him up really fast." Some girl had written in Italian on his wall. And I went crazy. I was like "What am I going to do? He is dating someone else. He is obviously attracted to her. He is writing on her wall. It's in Italian." So we had to go to a translating site to figure out what it actually said. Yes, this was such a task. And then we tried to look her up, but she had blocked her profile. So after class, we spent, I am not even exaggerating, maybe *two hours* Facebook stalking to figure out who her friends were, what exactly she looks like, if she did hang out with any other guys. And through all of this, we found out that she had a boyfriend and we got to his profile....Why did I spend two hours through someone else's profile to find out if this girl had a boyfriend so that my guy isn't dating someone else? That is exactly why I deleted Facebook.

It is relatively easy to find reasons to be suspicious of one's lover on Facebook—someone posts a flirty message on your lover's wall, or your lover is seen in photos that seem suggestive—but it is difficult to determine whether your lover is encouraging this flirtation or the context in which these photos were taken. Alan discussed the dilemma as he described his futile attempts to make his profile girlfriend-friendly:

> What I don't like about a picture is that it is physically shot, and you see what you see. But you don't know any of the background of what was going on at the time. You only see whatever you see in the picture. So you don't see if maybe this person didn't want to be in the picture, but they were forced to. You don't know if this person was maybe just walking by and someone said, "Hey, come get in this picture." All you see is that they were in the picture. So there was problems if I was in pictures with other girls, it would be posted under my photos, and Sarah would be upset about that. And I would try to untag these photos.[7] ... Untagging doesn't work because she can go look at their pictures, and see me in it, and see that I have untagged. So then that looks even worse.

Alan spoke to an important point about the partial knowledge Facebook provides—one never quite knows enough of the details. Other people I interviewed also talked about how photos can be inconclusive evidence; there are multiple interpretations of texts and images. Photos can be the smoking gun or they can reveal far too little about what happened just before and after the image was taken.

In addition, Facebook is a medium for displaying the self that one wishes one was, as people kept telling me over and over. Facebook profiles do not reflect who people are but who people want others to believe them to be. These profiles anticipate other people's gazes. Anticipating others' gazes implies two important components of

---

7. Photographs can be tagged with the names of the people in the photo. Untagging removes a person's name.

the Facebook checking that I am discussing. One can delete wall posts, untag photos, remove the "evidence." This can inspire people to search more diligently on Facebook for the evidence that the person under suspicion has not thought to delete—the accidental trace that may still linger in someone else's photo album who was also at the party. Alan gives an example:

> When the trust is not really there, Facebook is only your enemy. She would go look at my friends' photos. I can give you a good example. There was a huge fight because I have some good girl-friends who I am just friends with. I have always been just friends with them, nothing more.... I was at the bar and there were some pictures taken of all of us. And I decided to untag the photos. It wasn't a picture of me kissing a girl. It wasn't anything like that. Things were going very well, and I wanted to avoid an argument. And you know, maybe two weeks later, she is friends with them on Facebook, she happened to be looking through their pictures, and saw me in four of the pictures. "Why is Alan untagged from these pictures?" And then there is a whole fight.

In addition to creating a public persona, one creates and manages a Facebook profile for multiple audiences (see chapter 5 and Kendall 2007). Possible audiences include friends, one's lover, potential employers, professors, or family members. When people did not monitor their Facebook profiles to indicate that they were being considerate of their lovers, this too sent a message. Remember Olivia's ex-boyfriend, Brian, who was very sociable, and always had traces of how friendly and likeable he was on his Facebook profile. He was anticipating his friends' gaze but never seemed to take Olivia's gaze into account.

> That was one of the things I always told him, "You know, Brian, it says here 'in a relationship with Olivia.' Yet someone sees that and

goes to look at your pictures, and they are probably thinking, 'Well, is Olivia some kind of idiot?' because her boyfriend looks like some crazy insane guy with 8,000 girlfriends. I almost found it insulting, and I felt that it was degrading to me almost that he had these pictures. And it wasn't like these were naked pictures, but it was girls and girls and girls. And really not any pictures with me, I didn't use my digital camera. In our relationship, we never went "out-out" together all that much. We weren't in situations where you really take pictures, because generally you do that at the bars.

For Olivia, part of the problem was that he wasn't untagging photos or deleting flirty wall posts, and, at the same time, he wasn't properly signaling on his profile that he was in a relationship. Early in the relationship he was willing to be Facebook official (although that also changed over the course of their relationship). But he wasn't willing to do anything else to his profile to show others how important she was to him. She felt that he didn't care whether his Facebook profile would bother her.

As Alan mentioned earlier, untagging photos and deleting wall posts can also signal a warning to an anxious lover. Why would your lover be monitoring their Facebook profile—do they have something to hide, or are they being considerate of your feelings? As Alan further described the quandaries he fell into because of Facebook: "Do I leave this picture up and explain the best I can. Yes, I was with these people, they stopped for a picture. Or do I risk detagging the picture, and maybe it is never found. Or maybe the picture is found, and it looks a hundred times worse. Facebook poses these dilemmas." Part of the dilemma in reading a Facebook profile for insight into someone's actions is this lack of information about someone's intentions. One doesn't know why someone is leaving or deleting specific traces on Facebook. And this, after all, is precisely what the people I spoke to wanted to know—they were trying to use Facebook to understand another person's inner emotional life, not the actions they display for others. But all Facebook allows one to see is the actions displayed, not the thinking behind the display. Facebook's potato chips of information provide partial knowledge that leaves someone wanting more—wondering about the "why" and the context behind the traces of actions left on Facebook.

When analyzing how the structures of Facebook affect romantic relationships, I have to discuss the social interactions and expectations that people bring to Facebook. Facebook might refract these expectations, encouraging people to focus on one aspect of the information that their lovers are presenting to different audiences (which includes them, but typically is not exclusively aimed toward them). Technology is never outside of the social. But the material form of communicative media shape how and why people use them. The structure of technology matters—it shapes how knowledge will circulate and sometimes what kind of knowledge will circulate. But it doesn't determine how the technology will actually be used—only people can do that.

3

Remediation and Heartache

What happens if you start flirting with someone who refuses to text, or isn't on Facebook—in short, someone who doesn't use the same range of technologies that you do? Purnima faced this confusing issue one summer, when she was beginning to flirt with Ajay, who didn't use Facebook. Ajay kept phoning her and texting her; these were the casual ways he contacted people. Yet for Purnima, Facebook was the most casual way to contact someone, to begin to phone or text might be to indicate tacitly that you were interested in the person. So even though she knew very well that he was not on Facebook, she kept thinking that he was much more interested in her than she was in him every time he called or texted. Purnima had to remind herself that this really didn't mean anything more, that these media were his most informal ways to contact someone. Yet despite knowing better, she kept interpreting him as being really into her.

Purnima was faced with the contemporary dilemma of understanding someone else's media ideologies and practices in terms of the wide range of media choices the person has available to them. And while Purnima's use of texting and calling also depended on how she chose to use Facebook, this was not the case for Ajay, who was only choosing between texting and calling. Purnima was encountering *remediation*—how people's media ideologies and uses of one medium are always connected to people's media ideologies and uses of other older or newer media. Purnima was confronted with a practical consequence of the way remediation functions— not only do ideas about one medium shape the ways in which people use other media, but this interconnected set of media ideologies and practices can change from person to person, depending on their history with and use of different media. And these differences often present problems when someone tries to figure out another's motivations.

I only spoke with Purnima, so I don't know some important background for this brief story; namely, how Facebook might be spreading among Ajay's circle of friends. Ajay's history with different technologies remains a mystery. In the stories I tell, I discuss how different people are experiencing media.[1] Purnima and Ajay don't have access to every technology that has ever been invented, nor do they know about every technology invented.[2] People have personal experiences with how different technologies intertwine, and this connects with the ways these technologies are marketed and adopted in contrast to other technologies' circulation. People's media use is always affected by these histories of remediation.

1. There is, however, another approach one could take: one could focus on the larger histories surrounding the invention and distribution of a particular communicative technology in relation to the histories of other technologies' distributions. How an older communicative technology has been introduced and adopted often affects the ways people will use a more recently invented technology. The history of one medium's use shapes the histories of other media's use. While the history of different media is an important element of remediation, this is not what I focus on.

2. When I describe my research to people, I often have to explain Facebook, Twitter, World of Warcraft, or other media to listeners who are not familiar with these technologies.

To look at remediation, I look at how people use different technologies in conjunction with each other during breakups. Four aspects of remediation become important when people end relationships. First, when people compare media as they are breaking up, they tend to pay careful attention to how different media reveal other people's intentions or how different media store conversations. These comparisons affect the media they use in these moments. In other words, people's media ideologies are strongly affected by the comparisons people are constantly making between media, and this is an issue in breakups. Second, people are reevaluating what counts as a medium and are starting to assess in-person conversations as though they are mediated by technology. Third, when one takes remediation as a practice seriously, one has to pay attention to how and when people move from medium to medium. I analyze how the early stages of relationships as well as relationship endings are now shaped by how people move from one medium to another in an order that is supposed to reveal motivations and the seriousness of their statements. I conclude by discussing how people's reluctance or refusal to switch mediums shapes the ways in which relationships unfold as well.

A Medium Is Always a Comparison

To explore the ways people's use of one technology affects their use of other technologies, I draw on Jay Bolter's and Richard Grusin's 1999 book, *Remediation,* in which they argue that people's ideas and uses of recently introduced media need to be analyzed alongside people's ideas and uses of older media. Bolter and Grusin argue that new media never arrive on an empty stage; people always compare them with older media. Through these comparisons, people transform their understandings of both new and old media. What people understand a cell phone can accomplish, for example, is fundamentally linked to what a landline can accomplish (which wasn't called a landline until the introduction of cell phones), and now what a landline allows is understood also in terms of the cell phone's possibilities. Ideas about these media are mutually constitutive. "Our culture conceives of each medium or constellation of media as it responds to, redeploys, competes with, and reforms other media" (Bolter and Grusin 1999, 55). When new media are introduced, they are structured and understood in analogous relationships with previous media—think of how Web *pages* refer in their very name to books, or a CD's *liner notes* refers to how vinyl records are packaged. At the same time, ideas and uses about old media change as well. Listening to a record after the widespread marketing of digital audio players is a different experience, especially because digital players can play songs from different artists in random sequences. The user might notice that the songs are always in the same order on a record, a sequence that would be taken for granted before the advent of the digital player. Recently introduced media change people's ideologies and uses of old media as much as previous media influence new media.[3]

In terms of breakups, to understand people's experiences of being dumped by e-mail, one also has to understand the alternatives—what it would mean to be dumped by letter instead, as well as texting or voice-mail. Part of the reason remediation is so central to breakups is that there are currently so many options for transmitting the message "I want to break up." People's ideas about these media options are mutually defining. Some people dislike

3. An earlier version of this argument appeared in Ilana Gershon, "E-mail My Heart: Remediation and Romantic Breakups," *Anthropology Today* 24 (2008): 13–15.

text breakups more than e-mail breakups because there are only 160 characters available—how much can a person explain by text? Others prefer text-message breakups to e-mail because they do not regularly check their e-mail, so the breakup message could be waiting in their inbox for days. For both perspectives it is a question of e-mail *versus* texting. These evaluations invariably are about remediation, which is central to how people compare media.

When I initially began wondering whether studying mediated breakups might offer useful insights into people's experiences of these media as "new," I asked students in my courses about the relative inappropriateness of breaking up by Facebook, texting, and telephone. When I asked about the telephone, they were surprised by my own media ideology that phone was inappropriate. I thought of phone calls on the same level as texting—neither medium should be used to end a relationship. They disagreed. For my students, the telephone was just fine, especially if it was a long-distance relationship. I was a bit taken back that the telephone was so acceptable. It certainly was not when my friends and I were college students. When I told a couple I had known since undergraduate days that the phone was now acceptable for breaking up, they were surprised as well. The wife reminded her husband that in the mid-1990s, he had tried to break up with her over the telephone two days before she was to visit him in California from Taiwan, where she was living for the year. She said she went ahead and took that flight to California, her heart breaking across the Pacific, because she couldn't accept a telephone breakup. The visit did result in a breakup, however, and it took several years after this painful trip for them to reestablish a romantic relationship. This is just one example of how, when I was a student, telephones were to be avoided as a breakup medium if at all possible. Breaking up through any medium was considered inappropriate, and I recall other stories of people going to great lengths to ensure that they ended relationships face-to-face. Not so for many college students nowadays.

In subsequent interviews, other undergraduates have agreed with my class's sense that a phone breakup was almost, although not quite, equivalent to an in-person breakup. This is by no means every college student—some still found phone entirely unacceptable. Rachel, for example, explained at great length how inappropriate phone was.

> I think breaking up with someone on the phone is cowardly. It is a way to get out of a difficult situation that you don't feel like being in. I think that guilt was involved....It is childish. It is not taking responsibility for your actions and your behaviors and your decisions. It is easier to do.

Despite Rachel's vehement critique of phone breakups, she was willing to concede that phone was the second-best alternative, although far worse than face-to-face interaction, because one could have, as Rachel put it, "I say this, you say this" conversations. Students who found the phone acceptable talked about how much it approximates face-to-face communication, allowing for conversational turn-taking and intonation in ways other media do not. That many college students considered phone a reasonable alternative indicates they have a different history with various media than I do, as well as different media ideologies. When breaking up, they do not find the very fact of mediation unacceptable. Instead, they are concerned with the type of mediation. They interweave their media ideologies differently than I do. This change in attitude regarding whether the telephone was an acceptable breakup medium over the past fifteen or twenty years is a result of remediation. Two decades ago, people understood the main media options for breaking up to be face-to-face, letter, or telephone. Now the options are far more numerous, so people find the telephone a more desirable option than its many alternatives. As I have mentioned before, when college students discuss these many different options, face-to face interaction is always in the background, and students describe phone calls as the closest approximation to face-to-face conversation.

Yet as people are evaluating other media in terms of in-person communication, they are also reevaluating in-person communication in terms of these other media. People are beginning to reimagine what counts as a medium in general. College students are starting to describe face-to-face interaction as a medium, an option for communication with its pros and cons just like any other medium. This view often emerges in interviews when I discuss with undergraduates how new media have changed the ways in which knowledge circulates among friends and family. For example, I was interviewing Debra about how she responded to the announcements over the Facebook news feed that a friend of hers had just broken up. When she learned that her friend had broken up through the Facebook news feed, she was faced with a dilemma many Facebook users have had; namely, how best to acknowledge someone else's breakup? She was also very curious about what had actually happened, information the news feed did not convey. Debra told me that she was going to see if her friend (who went to university in another state) was coming home for Thanksgiving. She wanted to ask her friend about the breakup "on face-to-face." Even Debra's grammar indicates that face-to-face is becoming yet another medium for people. When people talk about the relative merits of different media for breaking up, they compare texting or instant messaging to in-person interactions as though face-to-face was just another medium. They talk about the importance of conversational turn-taking, of being able to ask questions, of hearing intonation, of offering a reasonably lengthy explanation. For them, face-to-face conversation is the ideal way to break up because it allows for the broadest bandwidth of information.[4]

Bolter and Grusin also argue that people evaluate media in terms of how a particular medium represents reality. For Bolter and Grusin, the question at the core of people's engagement with different media is how well and in what ways the media resemble reality. They claim that all media are evaluated as falling somewhere between two poles, the poles of immediacy and hypermediation (Bolter and Grusin 1999, 53–54). Some media, such as photographs, are compelling because of the perceived immediacy of their representation. People can believe that a photographic image bears such a strong resemblance to its subject that they can ignore some of the ways that it is a medium. For them, the photograph doesn't seem like a mediation; it is a representation that captures reality. Readers may have asked or been asked of a photograph: Do I really look like that? This question makes sense only if the people who are asking have a strong association between photographs and immediacy.

This association can be captivating. Courtney was one of many college students I interviewed who told me about the hours people might spend examining other people's photograph albums on Facebook: "My neighbor recently added my boyfriend as her friend, and she came in the next day and was talking about his pictures. She looked at every single picture. I was like, 'How do you do that all day?' Because she was referring to a picture like two years ago at prom, which is like hundreds of pictures back. But she went through all of them." Courtney's neighbor and other Facebook

---

4. No one used the metaphor of bandwidth in my interviews—this is an analogy inspired by Allucquère Rosanne Stone's *The War of Desire and Technology at the Close of the Mechanical Age* (1995).

photograph aficionados find photos fascinating because they assume that photographs show glimpses of reality. When the college students I interviewed talked about photos on Facebook, they do not describe photographs as altering reality through the ways that photographs capture a scene. That students presuppose that photos they examine accurately represent reality does not, of course, tell us much about how photographs depict a moment but only about how people understand them to function. Photographs are not inherently better at representing reality than other media, but people often consider photographs to be especially effective at capturing what *really* took place. This medium tends to fall squarely on the immediacy pole of Bolter's and Grusin's continuum between immediacy and hypermediation.

As Bolter and Grusin point out, not every medium seems to reflect reality. Some media are captivating because of *hypermediation*—when media calls attention to the act of mediation. Cartoons or video games are often examples of hypermediation. "[D]igital hypermedia," write Bolter and Grusin, "seek the real by multiplying mediation so as to create a feeling of fullness, a satiety of experience, which can be taken as reality" (1999, 53). Hypermediation is engaging because of the ways in which it gives the impression of providing a surplus of information—there is too much to observe—in much the same way, Bolter and Grusin argue, that one experiences unmediated moments. Some video games are compelling because there is too much going on, and so people have to choose what they want to focus on in much the same way that people have to pay attention in unmediated moments. Bolter and Grusin describe the continuum between immediacy and hypermediation as a range based on how one experiences representations' connection to reality. *Immediacy* gives the impression of mediating reality as little as possible. *Hypermediation* gives the impression of duplicating the ways people experience reality; the excess of stimulus forces the observer to be as selective as they are with unmediated experiences. For Bolter and Grusin, every medium is compelling because it offers a unique mix of immediacy or hypermediation. A medium is captivating because of how it moves from supposed transparency to calling attention to its influence in representing. Bolter and Grusin suggest that remediation revolves around the representation; that is, people evaluate a medium in terms of the ways in which it represents reality and the degree to which it duplicates people's sensory experiences.

In general, I found that people cared less about how a representation resembled their sensory experiences in the middle of a breakup than how a medium seemed to represent other people's intentions and feelings. Rachel's wish for "you say this, I say that" conversations might seem to support Bolter's and Grusin's claim that people are evaluating different media based on where a medium appears to be on the continuum between immediacy and hypermediation vis-à-vis all other media people use. When students talked about phones in terms of how closely a phone conversation can approximate an in-person conversation, this might seem to be a question of immediacy. I want to suggest, however, that this emphasis on immediacy and hypermediation is part of Bolter's and Grusin's own media ideologies, and that people care about different aspects of media depending on the context. I have found that questions of immediacy and hypermediation were relevant for remediation only when people were concerned with representing a concrete object or person. For the people I interviewed, how a medium linked representation to their sensory experiences of reality occasionally mattered. More often than not, they were far more concerned about the ways a particular medium could give insights into why another person did what they did—what another person was feeling and what motivated that person to act in a certain way. In short, accurate representations of a sensory reality were not as central an issue for the people I interviewed as accurate representations of intentions.

Deciphering the Why of a Breakup

When people are breaking up with each other, others' intentions—and their inscrutability—often are the dominant issue. Part of the reason people are privileging face-to-face breakups as the ideal way to end a relationship is because they want to know why; they want a reason that can sufficiently explain why the breakup is happening. They believe that face-to-face communication can lead to the conversations that will provide this and that other media are often inadequate to this task. A letter to online advice columnists Dan and Jennifer succinctly outlines how much people see face-to-face communication as the best way to gain some understanding of other people's intentions. The writer describes all the different media used to end a two-year relationship. His girlfriend broke up with him by e-mail while they were hundreds of miles apart. He tried calling her, but she refused to answer the phone. She was willing to text him back when he texted her, but only with vague, uninformative snippets of text. He finally decides he is going to visit her, both to pick up his things and to see if he can find out more about why the breakup has happened. He concludes: "To me I think I deserve to be able to talk to her face to face about all this. The way she broke it off with me just wasn't right. Anyone got any advice to how I should approach this when I get there?"[5]

5. See http://www.askdanandjennifer.com/love-relationships/breakup-and-divorce/breakup-how-to-never-argue-by-phone-or-e-mail/]

He has contact through at least three other media—e-mail, texts, and phone calls. But only face-to-face conversation will do as he tries to get an explanation that he finds adequate for why the relationship is ending. In the context of a breakup, seeking explanations of people's intentions dominates the interactions; how people are "actually" feeling and why they are doing what they are doing becomes the topic of many conversations, both between the couple and with their friends and family. As the advice-seeker's repeated mention of different media demonstrates, the media people are using to communicate become central to this process of determining others' intentions.

I do want to point out that in my interviews, as in this letter, reasons or intentions rarely sufficed, even in the interviews in which people seemed to know ostensibly why the breakup happened. Many people I interviewed, not only students, invariably felt unsatisfied, even those who were told reasons that on the surface might seem to provide the often elusive "closure."[6] Some people who were in the unpleasant position of being dumped talked about how much they wanted to understand what the other person was thinking or feeling in order to accept the breakup. Yet, as the one listening to many such breakup stories, I kept noticing that while they said they wanted explanations of a person's intentions, even when they heard an explanation, it rarely seemed to satisfy. People who had been broken up with sometimes kept searching for explanations and rejecting any explanations that were in fact offered. This sense of confusion and dissatisfaction could lead people to search for answers in ways they weren't proud of. They might break into their ex-lover's Facebook or e-mail accounts, or

6. An example of an explanation that did not satisfy: "I keep having panic attacks and don't feel mentally healthy enough to be with anyone right now."

monitor the traces of their ex-lover on Facebook or the Web. In these moments, they often talked about the ways in which different media can intertwine to help them figure out an ex-lover's reasons for acting in a particular way.

Katha Pollitt, a poet, writer, and activist, has written an engaging account of her own experiences of Web stalking in which she reflects on her temporarily insatiable search for insight into a recently ended relationship.[7] She searched the Web in the aftermath of the dissolution of a nine-year relationship as she tried to understand, although what precisely she was trying to understand remained elusive. She writes:

> At first, I felt guilty, as if somehow he could know. After all, if an e-mail program can tell you whether your message has been opened, maybe a search engine can tell you that someone is checking you out. Still, I would plug his name into Google, Lycos, HotBot, Alta Vista and up would pop, in distilled, allusive, elliptical form, like a haiku or a mathematical curve, everything I should have known: the life behind my life. Out of a soup or cloud composed of book reviews, publishers' notices, conference announcements, course assignments, Listserv postings, and tiny mentions and stray references embedded in documents devoted to some quite distant theme, a person would slowly condense, like someone approaching out of a fog who at first looks as if he were made out of fog, only darker. There on my screen glowed the programs of academic gatherings he had attended going back for a decade: the same female names appeared over and over entwined with his in panel announcements. (Pollitt 2007, 22)

All these different forms of transmitting information became intertwined for Pollitt as she searched for traces of her ex-lover in

---

7. My colleague Joan Hawkins brought Pollitt's book (2007) to my attention.

newspapers, academic journal articles, and so on. She began to piece together infidelities, uncovering who he might have slept with while they were together by interpreting academic conference programs next to her recollections of past phone calls and gifts. She searched for information on everyone in his life that she could remember him ever mentioning, trying to see through the traces of relationships on the Web some indication of how he conducted himself when she wasn't present. She did this for several months, staying up until one or two in the morning clicking through Web sites. Finally she found the Web site that freed her from what she describes as insanity. She came across real estate photos on the Web—his new girlfriend, her replacement, was selling her apartment. The photos reveal his collection of paintings, posters, and framed cartoons scattered throughout the apartment; he has reconstituted his life with another woman's generic apartment as the frame. Pollitt writes:

> There wasn't any point going on after that. I had found the magic Web site, the one that was a secret window into reality, but what did it show me that I didn't already know? What difference did it make what color their sofa was? In fact, what had any of my researches revealed that mattered in the end? I had proved to myself that the Internet was indeed a verbal map of the world, the set of propositions that were all that was the case, thrown over the physical world like a medieval rabbi's invisible cloak. But that was all it was. It could mirror facts and events, but not only could it not control or change them, it could not answer my real question: Why? (Pollitt 2007, 34)

Pollitt is freed by some photographs (collected on the Internet) of her ex-lover's casual life with another woman. But the photographs don't actually satisfy her—their glimpses into a reality of his collection of media forms, his framed cartoons and paintings, in a different context don't actually offer any explanations. It turns out that it isn't any understanding of intentions that frees Pollitt. What liberates her is the realization that nothing she finds, no words, no images, will ever offer her a sufficient explanation. And knowing that there is no closure for her through these means finally releases her from her compulsive search.

Media ideologies and remediation are essential components of these frustrated quests as people search for insights into their lovers' decisions. During and in the aftermath of breakups, people evaluate different media in terms of how accessible intentions are in a particular medium. Undergraduates in my interviews focus a great deal on whether a medium allows for conversational turn-taking (and thus is a better breakup medium) precisely because they claim that conversational turn-taking allows people to have better access to each other's intentions. They find follow-up questions invaluable. They would suggest to me that it is much harder to understand the reasons behind certain messages without being able to ask about the messages; certain media are understood to circulate information about intentions better than others. This is the axis along which breakup mediums are being remediated: not in terms of whether one medium seems more immediate or more hypermediated than another, but in how the medium circulates knowledge, and in particular, knowledge about that quotidian unknowable—how another thinks and feels.

As these remediations take place, what matters about the medium changes. While players of online role-playing games may still care deeply about how a particular game is a hypermediated experience of questing for gold, when they break up with each other in the game, they start caring far more about how the game's interface functions to reveal others' intentions.

Reading the Medium, Not the Message

Sometimes people focused on how their ex-lover was changing the media they used after a breakup to understand the ex-lover's intentions, instead of focusing on the actual messages sent. Q, a woman in her late thirties who was in the throes of a divorce, wasn't certain at first how serious her wife/ex-wife Isabella was about dissolving their relationship. She paid attention to when Isabella changed her passwords on various bank accounts or their joint Netflix (an online DVD rental company). She looked for telltale changes in Isabella's various social networking profiles, Facebook, MySpace, and other sites. She also asked friends to keep tabs on the apartment's answering machine, wondering when Isabella would remove Q's name from what had been a joint greeting. All these changes were underdetermined indications to Q about how resolved Isabella was to continue divorcing. Q mentioned that months later, Isabella still had not changed the answering machine's greeting to reflect the fact that they were no longer living together. What did this mean, Q wondered.

> My name is still on our home answering machine. And so if I call…I really want to know if it is still there. It is really impossible to call anyone anonymously these days. If I call, I know that it will be a missed call that I called. So I try not to do it. But, on the day after the election, I called. And she knew that I was down that day because she hadn't called. And I knew she would be at work. And I called the home number and I hadn't had verification for about a month that my name is still on the answering machine. And it is one of those things. In the beginning, my friends were like: yup, still there, you are still on the answering machine. But now, it is like four months later, I should be getting over this, I cannot be asking my friends to call the house to see if I am still on the answering machine. But I was down enough the day after the election, I had

enough reason to call....it gave me the mental space I needed to call the house, even though I knew she wasn't there, to hear that my name was still on the voice mail. And I don't know what the hell she is doing with that. But we are disentangling in all these other ways, but she hasn't taken my name off the answering machine. And this seems kind of old school. Ten, maybe fifteen years ago, that would have been important. Cell phones change that whole thing. Owning your own cell phone is totally different than the landline. You would never expect, like someone checking your voice mail on your cell phone, it's a breach of privacy. It's your phone. But the house phone is totally different. So the fact that she still has my name on the voice mail, it isn't that she thinks taking it off will hurt me, like changing the passwords. And I don't want to say: "What the hell, why is it on there?"

For Q, using media changes to interpret Isabella's intentions also involved figuring out how Isabella was involved in remediation as she changed the different intertwined technologies she could use to announce to others that a separation was occurring.

People don't focus only on how different media reveal intentions when they are evaluating a range of media in the context of breakups. They also judge media by how well a particular medium allows people to store conversations, thus allowing them to show these conversations to their friends.[8] College students will often describe how technologies allow people to store conversational exchanges and their media idealogies shape the ways in which people store conversations. In chapter 2, Rose talked about her cell phone's limited storage capacity for saving text messages when she is in the middle of a text-message fight. Others use their cell phone storage capacity to prepare themselves for an eventual breakup.

---

8. For other works on the links between remediation and storage, see van Dijck (2007) and Acland (2007).

For example, Summer told me that she began saving text messages from her boyfriend that she thought indicated that she should end the relationship. She planned to break up with him when she had collected a certain number of these messages.

> *Summer:* I did save the texts for a while. You know what ended up happening? Every time we got into a big argument, I stopped liking him less and less and less and less and less. After a while, it was "What the hell am I doing with him?" And I saved the texts that we got into an argument about. I started deleting all the good ones that he sent me, and I started saving highlights of the bad ones. The ones that he sent that really really hurt me, I would save all those…And when it gets to this point of number of texts, then I know that definitely it is time to break up. That kind of thing. When it gets to that number of texts, because this is like ridiculous.
>
> *Ilana:* What number?
>
> *Summer:* My phone says like a hundred or whatever, but I don't know how much it actually holds. I got to a good, like, ten texts that were really mean. It wasn't like the whole text, just like one segment of one part that just really pissed me off. And I just saved it there.

Summer was using her cell phone's storage capacity to decide when she should finally break up. When she had enough bad texts saved, it would be a sign that the time had come. But she was also keeping the messages to remind herself that she *should* break up, and to do this, she was using the way a cell phone shows on the screen how many messages have been saved before allowing the user to see the messages.

Technologies store messages differently depending on the structure of the technology. Texts are messages that are easily removed from the context of the conversation. For Summer, these context-less text messages were markers of the need to break up rather than markers of a particular fight. By contrast, when students save instant-message conversations, they keep the entire sequence of the conversation. Cell phones allow, and even encourage, people to save only what another person texted, not necessarily what they were responding to. This also affects how these conversations would circulate, as students showed (and sent) instant-message conversations or text messages to their friends and family as they asked for others' help in understanding and responding to the breakup. A conversation, and thus how people interpret a conversation, circulates differently through various media. People compare these different technologies in terms of how the technologies allowed them to store and circulate particular exchanges.

Changing Channels

Remediation affects how people switch from medium to medium, and how they understand the significance of switching media. In this section, I discuss how remediation affects not only people's media ideologies but also their practices. When do people cross easily between media, and when do they seem trapped in one medium? The significance of moving across media often came up in interviews when college women would tell me about the different media people used to flirt. People saw the decision to use Facebook, texting, or calling as signaling the stage of a flirtation or someone's interest. Texting, many college women insisted, was a medium that men used because it was so low stakes. Men would get a woman's phone number and then text instead of calling so as not to seem too interested. The degree of romantic interest was often seen as reflected in the medium someone chose for flirting. Yet there was not a shared consensus on what was the most casual medium for contact. Some saw texting as the way to initiate casual contact, others talked about choosing Facebook when they wanted to emphasize how casual the contact was meant to be. Students also talked about how switching from Facebook to texting (or texting to Facebook) marked for them a new stage in the flirtation, as did moving from texting to calling. People could be so conscious that switching media indicated a new stage of intimacy that they talked openly about not being ready yet to move from texting to calling. Jessie told me how her best friend had just been wrestling with this issue.

> My best friend actually has just gone through this awkward stage and they texted much more than they had been, like "What are you doing tonight?" It is kind of like a way of being like: "Okay, I am not going to get in the way of anything but I want you to know that I am going to talk to you." And the going back and forth—she was like: "It is so hard to explain yourself on text." So I asked: "Why not just call him?" "Oh no, we're not there yet." So it is like a whole new baby step. When the call used to be a big deal—"oh, he called me." Now it's—he texted me, then he called me, and now we are going on a date. Technology has become that new baby step between getting together.

Jessie and many others have noticed that the process of getting together is now a series of stages—stages that are often defined by the media used to communicate. To switch from texting to calling, as Jessie points out, can signal more seriousness in one's flirting.

Both getting together and breaking up often involve several different types of conversations. Sometimes people divided up these conversations across different media, using texting for one type of conversation and Facebook for another. Many people told me that they prefer texting to coordinate a meeting with someone or to find out quickly what someone was doing at that moment. They saw texting as useful for only limited exchanges of information. When they wanted a more intimate conversation, they would call or arrange to see the person. People could have a range of conversations with another person, each type of conversation shaped in part by the medium used. For example, Katie told me that a good friend of hers had recently told her by e-mail that he had a crush on her. She asked her friends and sisters what to do, and how to respond. She wanted to call him back and explain that she was starting to see someone else and didn't reciprocate his feelings. Everyone she asked recommended that she continue e-mailing him. They e-mailed a few times back and forth about this, and at the same time they saw each other in person and talked on the phone while they were e-mailing. But what they communicated about by e-mail stayed on e-mail. They never talked in person about anything they were actively discussing through another medium.

> *Katie:* With my friend who wrote that e-mail to me, I don't know if I respond back to him on e-mail, if I respond at all, or if I talk to him on the phone about it, or what to do. And it was almost a unanimous response [from my family and friends] like: respond in the same form, the same path of communication that he did. No one said to talk to him on the phone, everyone was like: "Well, he e-mailed you about it so I would just e-mail him about it."
>
> *Ilana:* Why did they think that?
>
> *Katie:* I don't know. Like I guess they just thought that if he wanted to talk about it on e-mail, then that is the form of communication that he wanted to leave it at. Which is kind of funny, like for the last week, because he e-mailed me like sometime last week. I replied to him on e-mail, and he replied back to me. And we were still talking on the phone, but we did not talk about it at all. So it was almost like a separation of two different sections of our friendship.

The fact that people have a wide range of media to choose from has allowed people to use different media for different types of conversations. People who are breaking up with each other have a wide range of conversations, some angry, some regretful, and some to indicate that yes, even though both people are hurt and angry, they still want to talk to each other. Q explained to me how she used both e-mail and texting to communicate with her wife/ex-wife, Isabella. Q had not wanted the divorce, and she wanted to let her soon to be ex-wife know exactly how miserable this decision made her. She used e-mail to let Isabella know about her emotions as she began to reckon with the consequences of Isabella's decisions.

Q: In general we communicate by e-mail.

Ilana: How does the e-mail work? Does the e-mail give you information that you then search for?

Q: Not usually....But in general the e-mail is legit, it's an actual form of communication. Now I am feeling a little bit better, but there was a time, just even a month ago, I guess. Well, a typical form of self-help would be to write down or to journal something, just to write it down, get it out of your head, just write it down. And what I would do is dash off a three-line e-mail and send it. Not really expecting a response. And realizing that this had an impact on her. Instead of writing down this thought in a journal, I was writing down this thought in a three line e-mail and immediately sending it.

And then the next time we spoke, she said: Honestly, I don't know how you expect me to respond to some of the e-mails that you send.

Q: I don't expect you to respond. I just want you to know what I am thinking.

And I fully expected her to say at some point: Please stop sending me those e-mails. But she hasn't.

While e-mail was a medium that Q used to communicate a wide range of emotions, but especially despair and hurt, texting was a medium in which she and Isabella discussed everyday details.

> *Q:* We did text. And if I text, she writes back almost immediately. And sometimes I was reading or like giving Jane [a friend] a live play-by-play of the texts that Isabella and I were texting. And she said: "It's so weird. I can't believe you guys have this kind of repartee over texting like right now when you are in the middle of trying to come to a financial agreement. The attitudes, or the comments are totally different."
>
> *Ilana:* I am fascinated. What do you mean?
>
> *Q:* I don't know if I have texts saved in my phone. I can't remember an example.... Okay, for example, this is maybe funny. She sent me a couple of boxes of winter clothes recently. I couldn't deal with them right away, I couldn't unpack them right away. And one day I realized I had no clean underwear. And instead of unpacking all the boxes, I am sitting in my pajamas, and my choice is to go through the boxes or to do laundry. But what do I do? I text Isabella "I am out of clean underwear. Are there any in those boxes?" And she wrote back right away. She wrote back within five minutes saying, "Sorry, I didn't clean out your underwear drawer." So we have that level of communication by text.

While Isabella did not always respond to Q's e-mails—they could be emotionally loaded after all—she always responded quickly to Q's texts. For Isabella and Q, text messages were safe and would not lead to the emotionally difficult conversations that phone calls and e-mails often became. To me, it sounded like the two had segregated the different types of disentangling conversations people often have, reserving texting as the medium to indicate connection, however banal.

Just as some technologies might be reserved for intimate conversations or low-key conversations, other technologies could be reserved for fighting. Students talked about how certain media, such as texting, led to fights, while others did not. While someone was in the midst of fighting by texting or instant messaging, they might be reluctant to switch media. Sometimes their friends encourage them to stick to a particular medium. Switching media, the friends argue, would put them in a position of weakness. Morgan explained how a friend of hers would get trapped in text-message fights with her boyfriend.

> *Morgan:* One of my best friends still uses text messaging all the time. So she will send—when she and her boyfriend are fighting—she'll send these really dramatic statements because she can. Because they kind of, they sound dramatic and stupid if you say them aloud, but if you send them over the text messaging, all of a sudden, it kind of, you know, it's still really dramatic, but she doesn't seem so silly, so she'll do it all the time. If she's mad at him, she'll say something really mean, but only [by text messaging] over her cell phone.
>
> *Ilana:* So does she check with you when she sends it?
>
> *Morgan:* Usually she calls me, and she's like: "and I said this to him, and he didn't even respond." Or then he said something equally mean back, and so, she never asks me if I think it's a good idea, because she knows I'll say no.
>
> ...
>
> She's like "Look what he just sent me. What am I supposed to say back?"
>
> And most of the time I'll [respond], "You should probably just call him, and you know, talk to him".
>
> And she's like, "Well, but what did he mean by that?"
>
> And I am like: "I don't know, you should ask him. On the phone."

Ilana: And that just doesn't work?

Morgan: Sometimes I can convince her that she should call him, and most of the time it was a misunderstanding. But sometimes, if we're there with my other friends, and they'll be like, "He said that? Well you should text him back and say, you know, you can call when you feel like it, I'm not calling you first or something. You can text message him back and say this."

Morgan believed that her friend needed to switch media to end the fight, and told other stories about how phone conversations or in-person conversations were in her eyes the only effective ways to resolve conflict. For her, refusing to switch mediums was also refusing to end the conflict. Morgan was not alone in her assessment. College students often described texting as trapping people into fighting.

Stuck in a Medium

People expected to use a range of media in the course of starting a relationship, but this did not always happen. Several college students told me about friends of theirs in high school who got trapped in texting-only relationships. The people who told me about this found it perplexing; they couldn't understand why their friends were unable to transfer the conversations into face-to-face communication.

Janine: But my friends senior year…their whole relationship or whatever might have been was via text, and like when they were together they didn't really talk that much. And they'd never really talk on the phone. I mean I guess when they were together they did talk, but it was just like all through text messaging, and it was, like they would be together and then they would leave, and then they would talk via text, and they wouldn't actually be talking as much when they were together.

It was really weird and she hated it. She was just like "Why can't he pick up the phone and call me? I don't feel like I can call him because like, all he does is text me."

Ilana: So what would that mean for her to call him if he is texting her?

Janine: I don't know, I felt like she thought it was awkward when they would talk, like actually talk over the phone or talk in person. But on text message he was like able to converse even though they were really stupid. Like it was just like they were the most impersonal conversations like on text, stuff like that. Like we'd see him at a weekend event, and then they would be texting, and it was just like "So did you have fun? So, like, how's your weekend going?" Like that kind of thing, just like not really real conversations.

Ilana: But they couldn't even do the not very real conversations face-to-face?

Janine: No, I mean, it was always really awkward. And like they even tried. Like they went out on a couple of dates, and stuff like that, and I think a couple of them were good, and then some of them were just really awkward. And then it just kind of continued via text. And it even went through, like, our semi-formal, which was sort of the equivalent of our homecoming, um, dance, like, she wanted to go with him? But this was all through text message so he never asked her 'cause I think he was too shy.

Janine had observed her friends who were trapped by texting and became increasingly puzzled about why they were so trapped by this. Even people who had been caught also told me how confused they were by the ways in which a medium seemed to trap them.

Trill told me about a relationship that had recently ended, one in which they seemed to communicate only by text.

Trill: Last semester I was kind of dating this guy. And at first it was just that we just happened to physically like each other. And we hung out all the time, and it was okay. We were like: "We don't really have feelings for each other, but…" But then we thought, maybe we should, you know, talk a little bit. And then it was a big issue because I always text. I mean, I have the biggest text problem, that is all I do, I text. It ended up not working out because basically, I couldn't talk to him face-to-face, like it was just easier for me to text. Like, I don't know, I would want to talk to him face to face, and I would approach him, like: "We need to go out, and have dinner or something." But he never would. And so I would be like: "Okay, I'll go back to texting." And so it was just easier that way. It wasn't the best because you can never tell how people are, how their emotions are. So it didn't work out very well.

Trill wanted to find a way to switch the channels of conversation, but she couldn't seem to find a way to do so. And the guy she was kind of dating wasn't cooperating; he wouldn't agree to go to dinner or any other activity where they were in public and expected to talk only to each other. This inability to communicate through multiple media is an exaggerated version of relegating some conversations to texting and other conversations to instant messaging and yet others to in-person conversations.

Sometimes the ways in which these students use media to demarcate the seriousness and the intimacy of a conversation makes switching conversations from texting to in-person conversation a switch with stakes that are too high. They are profoundly uncertain how serious they want to be. With this uncertainty in the background, moving into what they perceive as a more serious or intimate medium is being too explicit about how important the relationship could potentially become.

There is another reason why people might be reluctant or unwilling to change media: sometimes one has to learn how to interpret someone's ways of speaking anew. You might be used to figuring out what someone is trying to communicate by IM, but still not know how to interpret their moods and meaning by text, e-mail or face-to-face conversation. Audrey told me about a long-distance relationship in which it had been difficult to switch from communicating by IM to communicating in person.

> *Audrey:* I got into an argument, I guess we got into a fight and I didn't even know that we got into a fight. I thought we were just arguing. It was over something stupid, like that America is not the number 1 superpower. I don't know, I don't think America is going to stay the number 1 superpower; I think we could easily lose that to someone else. He is in the army, and I am a little more liberal and I think that other countries have the vast technology....He is army and pro-America.
>
> *Ilana:* When was this? Was this on the phone?
>
> *Audrey:* This was in person. I wasn't used to it because I thought we were just having a discussion. And he was really mad, and he strode off. And I went "wait, are we in a fight?" And yes, we were. We were in a fight, and I had no idea. You can talk to someone online but you don't get the emotional inflection. Sometimes if you know them really well you can hear them saying those things. And sometimes you get the emotional inflections between the way they write and the speed at which they write it or, like, the phrasing. Like you can actually pick up the emotional things behind it....I didn't know he was fighting with me because we had never had an argument before, at least in person. Yes, online, but typing and physical gestures are two different things.

As Audrey points out, over time people develop patterns for communicating with each other in a particular medium through familiarity and some shorthand. She found out through arguing in person that for her, this familiarity and shorthand was inextricably linked to instant messaging. When Audrey and her then-boyfriend switched mediums, they had to learn all over again some strategies for interpreting what the other person was feeling or trying to communicate. In short, switching media might be a problem because it involved learning to communicate with someone all over again.

The examples above involve people who are trying to switch between different media, but not as fluidly or successfully as they wish they could. In breaking up, however, sometimes people refused to switch media. Before I had any inkling that I might want to write about mediated breakups, I had an experience with a text breakup in one of my classes. I was showing a film clip, and as I went to dim the lights, I realized that one of my students, Rebecca, was on the verge of tears. I asked her if she was all right while the film clip distracted the rest of the class, and she told me that her boyfriend had just texted her that he wanted to break up. I told her to go home; we both knew she could not concentrate in class after that happened. This was all I knew for a while. Later, when I started interviewing people for this project, Rebecca generously told me what had happened that day two years earlier. She talked about how her boyfriend decided to text her that he wanted to break up out of the blue and then refused to talk to her on the phone when she called him.

> *Rebecca:* This is all over text. I hadn't talked to him since a week before we broke up, until four months after we broke up. We didn't speak. It was all text messaging.
>
> *Ilana:* So why didn't you call him?
>
> *Rebecca:* I did. He wouldn't answer. He doesn't answer the phone. And I said, like: "How are you going to do this? We need to talk. Like you can't just end it like this, this is ridiculous."
>
> And he was like: "I can't talk to you now," or whatever. "It wouldn't make anything better. You wouldn't change my mind."
>
> And so that pissed me off.
>
> "I am not trying to change your mind, I am trying to understand what is going on."

In this instance, Rebecca's boyfriend was refusing to switch media in order to ensure that the breakup lasted. As Rebecca described later in the interview, when they had teetered on the brink of ending the relationship before this, they would talk, and by talking would find a way out of breaking up. By only texting, he was ensuring that the breakup took place.

Rebecca's story is not typical—most breakups I heard about took place over a range of media. A few people over thirty did tell me other stories about their partners who refused to move from e-mailing to talking. In every case, this refusal seemed to be a conscious decision to ensure that the breakup actually happened. These couples had been caught in cycles of breaking up and getting back together. Rebecca and the others in her situation whom I interviewed were all acutely aware that refusing to switch mediums was an active choice on the part of the person breaking off the relationship. This decision prevented reconciliation. Both switching media and refusing to switch media can affect how a breakup will unfold.

People's media ideologies affect which media they use, when they use a particular medium, and how they interpret using different media to end relationships. I have been expanding Bolter's and Grusin's concept of remediation to include a set of intertwined media ideologies in which ideologies about old media and new media mutually shape each other. As people encounter new media, their ideas about what counts as a medium may change—in particular, people may start thinking about in-person interactions in terms of a medium that conveys the most information. Bolter's and Grusin's focus on media as vehicles for representing sensory experiences seems too narrow to capture the many ways in which people evaluate when and how media affect communication.

Remediation affects practice. Part of understanding remediation involves understanding that people use a range of media—and not always the same range. The use of one medium is always affected by the other media a person uses regularly, as well as the media they refuse to use. Some communicative tasks, such as becoming a couple or breaking up, often end up involving the use of multiple media. These are moments when people consciously put their own understandings of remediation, of how different media intertwine, into practice. They are often also using their media ideologies as they wonder whether different media can reveal other people's intentions. When analyzing practices of remediation, one should notice when people refuse to allow media to intertwine by refusing to switch media or by insisting on having certain kinds of conversations only in a particular medium. This is just as important as noticing what media they choose. In these ways, remediation is at heart of contemporary breakups.

4

How Do You Know?

Mary Anne said that the breakup fight began because a good friend of hers had posted the Backstreet Boys' video, "Get Another Boyfriend," to her Facebook wall. Her boyfriend saw this and became angry that she was talking about the problems in their relationship with her friends, and, in particular, this friend.

> *Mary Anne:* I was dating this guy [Ryan] for a month and a half, and he was long-distance. He lived in Philadelphia, and I lived here [in Indiana], obviously. And Jason, my best friend, Jason has been my best friend since I was fifteen years old. Like he is also long-distance, we all met at this summer camp when we were growing up. And we worked together as counselors this past summer....So Ryan and I were dating, and we had been having some issues. We were fighting about really stupid stuff. I went out to visit him [in Philadelphia], and there was no chemistry anymore. I hung out with Jason the whole time, which Ryan being the idiot that he is, invited Jason along to everything because they live right by each other. So, the next week, when I come back and Ryan and I are trying to work out our issues, Jason posts on my wall a YouTube clip of [the] "Get Another Boyfriend"...video. And so Ryan, knowing that Jason has had feelings for me in the past and knowing my history, was like: "What's behind this? What's behind this?" And so we ended up breaking up.

Ilana: Wait, you broke up over the video?

Mary Anne: No, it started the discussion that led to us breaking up. Like, there was a lot of things that were going on. Without the video we would have probably broken up anyway. But that was the initial "Why does your Facebook say 'get another boyfriend'?"…

Ilana: So you didn't post the video.

Mary Anne: No, Jason posted it on my wall.

Ilana: So why was Ryan having problems with this?

Mary Anne: Because he knew that I had to have been talking with Jason about my issues with Ryan for Jason to be ready to put something like that on my Facebook wall as "Get Another Boyfriend." He [Jason] meant it like it could be funny or oh, take it seriously. And he said to me on the phone: "You just need to get another guy, or get another boyfriend." He thought it was really funny, and he posted it on my wall.

Ryan was angry about the context and conversations that the posted video implied, and he took away from that wall post much more information than simply "someone posted a Backstreet Boys' video to my girlfriend's wall."

All this information was second-order information, including assumptions about conversations his soon-to-be-ex-girlfriend was having with someone who disapproved of their relationship and wanted to date her himself. *Second-order information* is not what is actually said but rather the background knowledge of a situation and expectations of communication that allows one to interpret the words. Second-order information accompanies the exact phrases in the message itself, and guides people in how to interpret others' actions and intentions. Breakup stories are filled with instances in which people are interpreting second-order information, using what they know about the act of sending the message and the medium through which it is sent to interpret what is actually typed or said. During breakups, people are often interpreting second-order information to understand what other people's motivations are and how information about the relationship is circulating.

Breakups often present social dilemmas, which can be exacerbated when people don't share common understandings about the kinds of second-order information different media provide. Every medium offers second-order information differently, in part because of the structures of that technology and in part because of people's media ideologies. As people use new media, they have to develop strategies for interpreting the way a particular medium presents second-order information. When people are consciously evaluating second-order information, they are often trying to figure out the sender's intentions or what the second-order information can indicate about the context in which the message was sent. Sometimes they are trying to control what is revealed about their own intentions. In my interviews, people were also focused on trying to figure out how information was circulating; that is, who knows what, and how to navigate the tangle of "I know you know that I know that you know." While people were concerned about other people's intentions, they were as concerned with how to use new technologies to reveal or conceal that they knew something and why they knew it.

Interpreting intentions and determining who knows what are often intertwined tasks. For example, sometimes second-order information is circulated by the design of the technology without anyone actively sending a message. Facebook lets people know that someone is logging on to their profile with their password while they are online because only one user can access a profile at a time. If you are on Facebook and someone else logs on to your profile account, you are immediately kicked off of Facebook. This can be useful information. If you get booted from your own account, it may indicate that your ex-lover has figured out your Facebook password and is checking your account regularly. This also means that your ex-lover is still emotionally entangled. In this and other cases, knowing that someone wants to know also seems to reveal useful insight into their feelings and motivations. As people use media ideologies to understand how technologies affect their conversations, part of what they are interpreting is the second-order information that the structure of a particular technology provides, what this indicates about how people are circulating knowledge, and how intentional the second-order information might be.

Away Messages

Both during and after a breakup, people often try to use second-order information to communicate their feelings and motivations to their exes and friends. An away message is a message the user composes that will appear when they are contacted by someone but not logged on to their instant messenger (IM) profile. Away messages are a common vehicle for second-order information. People described quoting lyrics from songs on their away messages on their instant messenger (IM) profile or posting song videos on their Facebook walls in an attempt to let others know how they were feeling, without having actually written the words themselves. By quoting the words, they are consciously implying that the feelings expressed by the words are their feelings as well. But they might also decide to deny that the words reflected their feelings by talking instead about how much they liked the lyrics aesthetically. When Rachel's boyfriend began to break up with her, she was very upset and used her Facebook profile to express her anger and sadness. As she began to get used to the breakup, this was also reflected on her Facebook profile.

> *Rachel:* Wednesday night, he text messaged me and he was like: "Would you want to do laundry tomorrow sometime?" And at the end it's like: "I hope it's not too late," because I had just put a frickin' song up on my Facebook, it's called "You Could Be Happy," and it's all about people breaking up.
>
> *Ilana:* So you were letting him know by Facebook?
>
> *Rachel:* Kind of. It's just a really great song, because it's like: You weren't happy when you left, but the thing I want for you is to be happy, even if I'm not there. I want you to do really great.

After Rachel posted the song, her soon-to-be-ex-boyfriend saw this as a sign that she was starting to accept the breakup and might be willing to spend time with him without being angry or offering recriminations. The song itself contained the message that Rachel ambivalently wanted to send,[1] so that posting the song made it seem as if she was taking responsibility for the sentiments the song expressed. Posting the song on Facebook was sending a second-order message to her soon-to-be ex.

People also talked in detail about how they used their instant message (IM) away messages to communicate how they were feeling. Some of the students I interviewed believed there was a strong gender divide in the ways people used IM away messages after a breakup: women, they said, tended to use lyrics or quotes about how strong they were and how well they were surviving the breakup. Men tended to describe the activities that were taking them away from their computers, such as football games or classes. Rose decided to

---

1. She might have been starting to accept the breakup, but she clearly was still very angry at him when we talked.

prepare for the interview with me by collecting the IM away messages of various friends of hers.

> *Rose:* When girls break up, or when boys break up, on IM you can put up an away message, and you also have profile stuff. I printed off the away messages of the girls that I know that have broken up or been broken up with over the last six months, and the two guys that have been broken up with over the last six months. And if you look at the girls, they are from different colleges, some of them don't know each other, and you read what their profile on AIM [AOL Instant Messaging] says, they are all, like, interestingly almost similar to each other. "Everything happens for a reason. People change so that you can learn to let go. Things go wrong so that you can appreciate them when they go right. You believe the lies so you eventually learn to trust no one but yourself. And sometimes good things fall apart so better things can fall together."[2] This is one of the girl's.

> *Ilana:* Her away message?

> *Rose:* Yes.

> *Ilana:* It is all about "I just got dumped and I am trying to recover."

> *Rose:* Right, and here is another one: "Life is too short to wake up in the morning with regrets." These two girls have never met. "So love the ones who treat you right, and forget the ones that don't. And believe that everything happens for a reason. If you get a chance, take it. If it changes your life, let it. No one said it would be easy. They just promised it would be worth it." They are all similar like that.... The men are all like, "Football game tonight, can't wait."... The girls are for, I think, it is so that the guy will look at them or something. I don't know why you would do that. Do you have any ideas? It is constant with all the girls I know who have broken up, these heartfelt, poured out, "I am strong,

2. This quote has been widely attributed to Marilyn Monroe.

I am going to get through this, I am going to be okay. This is going to make me a better person" kind of thing.

In borrowing other people's words, Rose's female friends tended to try to send second-order information that they were independent and thriving, no matter how heart-broken they felt. Rose's male friends seemed to ignore the breakup entirely in their away messages.

While men in Rose's circle of friends would not indicate any sign of heartache through their away messages, this was not the case for all men. Other women told me that after they had decided to break off a relationship, their ex-boyfriends would use away messages or Facebook status updates as platforms to express their misery. These men used lyrics on their away messages to portray themselves as devastated.

> *Anne:* He probably had bad quotes on there for a couple months. Now that I think about it, it was like two months. It was a long time, a long, long time. I had gotten to the point where a friend would ask: "Did you see his message?" [And I would reply] "Yeah, typical, no big deal. Get over it." I guess he just updated his status to do that. We didn't talk until a year and a half [after the breakup]. It was a while; it was really hardcore. And then I started dating someone else, and I obviously didn't want to say I was in a relationship, because I didn't want him to see it. I didn't put any pictures of us up, because news feed announces that I have updated my photos, and then he can see it. So you have to be careful what you put on it, untag stuff. People know then that there is a new person in your life, and go "Who's that guy?" And then he would know that too. Then there would be another round of bad quotes that I would have to deal with. So I was essentially shaping what I was doing through Facebook so he wouldn't have to know.

> *Ilana:* What did your friends say about this?

Anne: At first, they felt really bad for him. Because he seemed really sad and he seemed really upset. But then eventually, it became "Seriously, you have to stop the messages." I wish I could remember some of them, they were so intense. They were terrible, long, like think of the worst country song you could imagine. It was pretty much that, everywhere, all the time.

Ilana: And was he always quoting other people?

Anne: Yes.

In both instances, men and women were using other people's words to communicate with their exes, assuming that even if their ex did not see the away message themselves, their friends would notice.

Anne also started worrying about how information she posted would affect her ex. His melodramatic quotes started to have an impact on what she was willing to indicate, even indirectly, on her Facebook profile. As her ex kept broadcasting his broken heart through his Facebook status updates, she kept avoiding posting any sign that she might be in a new relationship or that she had moved on. Part of the work of breaking up, in these instances, was managing not only the direct communication but also the second-order information that messages contain.

This widespread tendency to use lyrics and quotes as ways to communicate one's own emotions can sometimes frustrate people who don't wish to use their away messages or status updates in this fashion. Other people will interpret these messages as insights into someone's emotional state, whether or not the away messages are intended to be read in this way. Halle explained that away messages had become a continual headache for her.

Halle: Away messages! Bad news bears! Away messages are trou-u-u-ble.

Ilana: What did away messages do to you?

Halle: Well, basically, you put up an away message and people read in it, like it is a novel.

Ilana: So what kind of away messages did you put up?

Halle: Okay, so I am a huge music fan. I am one of those people who has a cooking playlist, and a cleaning playlist, and a going-to-bed playlist, and a getting-up playlist, and a getting ready playlist. I do everything with music. And I really like lyrics. So I put up lyrics all the time. Because I find rhymes interesting, and I find double entendres interesting, I love it. Well, people think that they [the lyrics] are all talking about me, or they are all talking about them. Everyone thinks that your away message is speaking to *them.*

"Are you mad at me?"

"What??!? No, I was just listening to this song."

"No, you are mad at me."

"No, I'm not. Sorry to disappoint you."

Away messages are so bad.

For Halle, it seemed impossible not to have people interpret her away messages as containing second-order information until she began to quote television shows on her away message instead of song lyrics. I asked her how people knew that these were quotes from a television show, and she said that she would also include the character's name who said the line in the displayed text. Halle found that away messages required a bit more extra effort as she tried to anticipate potential misreadings of her away messages—a task she found a bit ridiculous.

Second-Order Newness

Many of the social dilemmas that people face when they use new technologies involve interpreting second-order information.

It is often hard to determine whether people actually intend to send the second-order information that their message or lack of message appears to contain. What should you think when someone hasn't yet accepted you as a friend on Facebook? Maybe they haven't checked their Facebook recently. Maybe they are overwhelmed with requests. Maybe they are lazy. Or maybe they don't like you and don't want you to have access to their profile. Some of these social quandaries revolve around how to interpret information, such as interpreting why someone hasn't friended you yet. Debra talked about how changes in Facebook had created all sorts of new dilemmas in terms of the second-order information that was now regularly circulated.

> *Debra:* With the news feed now, it says when you friended them. It used to be that when Facebook first started, when someone friended you, you could be like: "Okay, I don't want to be friends with you." And you could not friend them, and they would never know, unless they checked to see if you were friends later. But who has that much time? But then with the new one, if someone friends you and you don't friend them, it won't show up in the news feed.

As Debra points out, as technologies change their interface or structure, the kinds of second-order information they can reveal changes as well. While in a previous Facebook interface, people had to actively look for signs that their friendship request was not accepted, now they know their request was refused because the news feed otherwise would let them know it had been accepted. For Debra, this gave her new possible ways to insult people that she now had to try to avoid; it was now more noticeable when she wasn't interested in being friends with someone. Yet the people noticing whether or not Debra was friending them were also faced with a new dilemma: Do they acknowledge that they have noticed? Letting someone know that you have paid attention to their decision to friend you might be revealing that you care too much about what they think of you.

While interviewees spent quite a bit of time discussing how to interpret other people's friending practices, they spent even more time talking about how complicated it was to interpret someone else's relationship status. If there is no relationship status, does this mean they are not in a relationship or that they simply don't want to tell others on Facebook about their love life? If a woman is in a relationship with another woman, is she gay, or is this a good friend of hers who is serving as a placeholder on Facebook? The relationship status on Facebook showed, for many, ambiguous information; it often wasn't clear precisely what someone was trying to indicate with the relationship status they had chosen. This was largely because people had different idioms of practice surrounding relationship statuses and different groups of people had developed their own agreed-on ways for communicating with relationship statuses. Some people used the relationship status to indicate when their relationship was official; that is, Facebook official. Others, however, marked that they were in a relationship by removing the status entirely.

> *Lucy:* When we first started dating, I wasn't sure if I wanted to be in a relationship when we just met. So we decided that we were not going to label anything until we were completely comfortable with each other. So no label on Facebook. [Her relationship status on Facebook was "single" during this period.] We didn't have a label with our friends or anything. We dated, and then we got to the point where we realized we are pretty much exclusive, and we act like a couple, so why not? So I wanted to take off "single" on my profile so I wouldn't be misleading anyone else.

So I just took it [the relationship status category] off, and he just took it off. It doesn't say in a relationship with anyone. Both of us just have that whole line taken off.

Lucy and her boyfriend changed their relationship status on Facebook when their relationship became more serious, based on an agreed-on commitment. They weren't simply changing their relationships *to* something. Still others refused to offer any indication about their romantic life on Facebook. Some people joke through their relationship status by being "married to" a Japanese movie star[3] or a best friend; others take it all too seriously. Interpreting what the relationship status indicates about someone's offline relationship status takes additional research—Facebook statuses can not be relied on as accurate. This can drive people to consult their friends about how to best interpret a profile. As the Gunslinger explained:

A couple of girls I was interested in, I looked on their page, and it just said interested in friendship or it had nothing. It didn't say relationship status or anything. I was talking with a friend of mine, and she said it either means that she is in a relationship with someone who isn't on Facebook, or they are genuinely interested in friendship and they aren't looking for a relationship. Then of course that sends me to look at all their pictures to see if I can find someone who is recurring, or I will look through their wall posts for recurring wall posts, but boyfriends and girlfriends don't write on each others' walls.

3. When I asked a student very active in the Mormon Church whether her friends posted that they were married to their best friends on Facebook, she said this was not acceptable. Her friends worried that it might imply that they were queer. Instead, her friends created fake Facebook profiles of their favorite Japanese movie stars and would post through their Facebook relationship status that they were "married to" the star.

The relationship category "it's complicated" exemplifies how underdetermined relationship status information can be. No one quite knows what it means. People have started to develop some strong hunches based on how those around them seem to use the term. Many of the people I interviewed thought "it's complicated" indicated problems in the relationship, that it was one of the first public indications on Facebook that a breakup might be imminent. Others, however, use "it's complicated" to convey a different message. When one student put "it's complicated" to indicate that she was in a long-distance relationship with someone she met during her overseas study in Greece, acquaintances on campus kept asking her if they were still together. She was trying to use "it's complicated" to indicate the headaches of a cross-Atlantic relationship, but other students' first inclination was to interpret the status as marking a relationship that was falling apart.

Another woman told me that when she first arrived on campus, as a freshman, she became casually involved with a resident assistant (RA) in her dorm (but not on her floor). They never were "in a relationship," but they posted "it's complicated" on Facebook to indicate that they were in the beginning stages of a relationship, which might or might not progress toward "in a relationship" on Facebook.

> *Rosie:* Our Facebook accounts did say "it's complicated with" and then we had each other on there.
>
> *Ilana:* You had "it's complicated"? So why did you decide to have "it's complicated"?
>
> *Rosie:* Because at that point in time we were sort of friends with benefits, but we were kind of dating.
>
> *Ilana:* That is so interesting. You are the first person who has told me about having "it's complicated" not meaning "we are on the verge of breaking up."

Rosie: I think it's kind of a bell curve. You use it on the way up, and you use it on the way down.

Ilana: People have been really clear with me that they don't use it on the way up.

Rosie: See, I did.

Ilana: That's fine, but this is really a different practice.

Rosie: I am trying to think about why I did it.

Ilana: Were you the one deciding to do it, or was he the one deciding to do it?

Rosie: I want to say that I am the one who wanted to put something on Facebook, and he's the one who wanted "it's complicated." I am sure I went along with it because it's not like we were really dating.

As Rosie points out, the choice of which relationship status to use can be a negotiated question, although more often people described the negotiation as surrounding whether to post a linked relationship status in the first place. These negotiations between the couple were always done with a sense of what everyone else around them seemed to expect. In this case, Rosie thought that her older non-boyfriend had a better sense of when people used "it's complicated" in college than she did. Part of the work of moving to a new place or joining a new group of friends was learning or deciding together what the agreed-on ways of using the Facebook relationship status and other features of new technologies would be.

The Relationship Talk and the Relationship Status

Taking the relationship status seriously often shaped the ways in which relationships would unfold. Often people don't quite know when a relationship begins. The college students I interviewed wondered about questions that may be familiar to others in new relationships, such as: Does the other person like me? How much does the other person like me? Is this casual? Is this serious? What do I want to happen? What does the other person want? For decades, college students have been resolving these questions with The Relationship Talk—a ritual moment in which people embarking on a relationship clarify the terms of the relationship. A 2008 column by Jamie Wiebe in Northwestern's student newspaper described the parameters of "the Talk":

> "The Talk" is easily the most awkward and uncomfortable part of a burgeoning relationship: You're in those lovely, early stages and things are great but you or your lover want to know "where things are going."…There's no need to force your relationship to fit one of Facebook's labels. There are a million random combinations of restrictions, requests and requirements that make up functional romantic partnerships. Try to reach a compromise that includes both parties' wants and needs. But don't agree to any conditions you can't commit to just because you like the person. Consider this: Is there still the possibility of a traditional relationship? Will you go on dates? Can you tell friends you're dating?
>
> Although this approach allows for the most flexibility, it's easy to get caught up in the details and forget to mention something you wanted. Before making a decision, make sure you've covered all your bases (not those ones); otherwise, prepare for a few sleepless nights pondering the specifics.[4]

Wiebe stresses the ways in which the relationship talk is a contractual conversation, one in which the rules of the relationship are ex-

---

4. Jamie Wiebe, "Where Is Your Relationship Going? Having 'The Talk.'" January 31, 2008. http://www.northbynorthwestern.com/2008/01/6576/thebigtalk.

plicitly spelled out. She also mentions the ways in which Facebook is beginning to shape the relationship talk, suggesting that one does not have to define oneself vis-à-vis Facebook categories. Yet the Facebook relationship status possibility does more than simply offer a limited menu of possible romantic configurations; it also offers another avenue for entering into—or circumventing—the relationship talk.

People can now use a discussion of their relationship status on Facebook to stand in for the contractual conversations that often occur in Relationship Talks. People can circumvent the relationship talk entirely by sending a "in a relationship request" to someone. The Facebook relationship status request sometimes allows people to avoid the Talk, but one can avoid the Talk without using new media as well. For example, one can introduce one's new boyfriend or girlfriend to friends as one's new lover (letting the new lover know at the same time as the friends).

> *Halle:* I started to date someone. And I got an e-mail saying "so-and-so says you are in a relationship. Confirm?"
>
> *Ilana:* Did you talk to the new guy you were dating about whether to put it on Facebook?
>
> *Halle:* Well, I mean, you go on dates, and then you are dating. You meet the parents and everything. We had been dating at this point, and it was like two months, something like that.
>
> *Ilana:* Had you had a relationship talk?
>
> *Halle:* He had introduced me to his friends as his girlfriend. I have always found this a very interesting way to do it, because it kind of surprises you as well as his friends. You find out at the same time as his friends do.

Others found that sending a relationship request by Facebook without discussing it first was a risky strategy. One woman I spoke to wanted to determine how serious a guy whom she was dating was about her. She didn't think they were in a relationship, but she wanted to know what he thought was going on.

> *Ilana:* Do you have a talk, or do you just try and put it on Facebook?
>
> *Noelle:* I try to just put it on Facebook. It had negative come-back, or feedback or something. I was dating someone, and so I sent a relationship request on Facebook. But it didn't get accepted.
>
> *Ilana:* Oh. What did you do?
>
> *Noelle:* Nothing.
>
> *Ilana:* Did you talk about it at all?
>
> *Noelle:* Mnh—mnh [no].
>
> *Ilana:* Did you break up?
>
> *Noelle:* No. We just kept talking. But he wouldn't put it on Facebook.

Her request was a direct claim that they were in a relationship, but she was also trying to figure out a question that involved second-order information—what about the relationship was he willing to declare publicly? Accepting her request would indicate not only whether they were in a relationship but also whether he was willing to tell everyone in their Facebook networks that they were in a relationship. When he turned her down, they never spoke about this decision face to face. They continued talking for a while longer, but their interactions soon petered out, in part because she and her friends suspected that he was trying to hide something. His unwillingness to publicly acknowledge the relationship was a clue for her.

People can also use discussing whether or not to change the Facebook relationship status as a substitute for discussing the complicated questions of what each person wants. Keeping the conversation contained by focusing on whether to become Facebook official allows many of the assumptions about what it means to be in a relationship to remain implicit. People can have different definitions of what "in a relationship" means or, as discussed earlier, what "it's complicated" means. Talking only about the Facebook status, and not the assumptions each holds about what that status signifies, can allow people to circumvent the more contractual and definitional aspects of The Relationship Talk.

Changing one's relationship status to indicate the end of the relationship can also create a surprising number of social dilemmas. As I mentioned before, ending a relationship on Facebook does not always mean the relationship is over. People can move rapidly through the various categories in a day, a week, or a couple of weeks as relationships are redefined, shifting from "in a relationship" to "it's complicated" to "single," and back to "in a relationship."

> *Frank:* It's kind of weird because Maria and I broke up three times in February, like off and on, off and on. And it got to the point that people would see it happen through the news feed on Facebook that 11 p.m. we had broken up and that at 6 a.m. we had gotten back together. They were like "What the hell is going on with you two?" And I would be like: "You don't want to know. It's just a mess."

Changing the relationship status can become a way to signal to one's lover how one is experiencing a fight, not necessarily signaling to one's Facebook network that one's relationship is over. As I mentioned in chapter 1, some students were so used to this strategy among their group of friends that they would not believe a Facebook breakup declaration until a week or so had passed without a reconciliation.

For Audrey, although she and Brad declared that the relationship was over on Facebook, it took more than that before she knew that the relationship with Brad had truly ended. Her family and friends thought that they were experiencing a momentary break and would be able to resolve their differences and get back together.

> *Audrey:* And then you have the news feed that says Brad is now in a relationship with June. And it says the whole name. And my friends, right when I checked it, it was kind of humorous. My roommate, one of my best friends, came running. And was like "you know already." Because my other roommate called her and was like: "Find Audrey. She is not going to be okay in like ten seconds. Go find her and make sure she is okay. Because this is going to hurt." Because it was not even a month after he ended it. So obviously.
>
> *Ilana:* Not even a month?
>
> *Audrey:* We ended on New Years, so I guess it was a month. But we had been talking for a few weeks afterwards. Because everyone thought we would be back together. All of us were like "Don't worry, you'll be back together soon." No one knew why he did this. He didn't tell any of his friends. I had phone calls from his friends "Don't worry." His sister was like "Audrey, this is impossible. It was like two days ago he told me how much he liked you. You guys are going to be back together as though nothing happened. You guys don't even fight. Don't worry, it will all be fine." Everyone, his mother, all his friends, were saying, "This isn't going to last. This isn't going to last." Well then...I was like: "I don't know, I don't think this is right. I think this is over. I don't know." And then all of a sudden, on Valentine's Day, it said officially "in a relationship." And they have been in a relationship ever since.

The true end was signaled only when Brad announced he was in a relationship with someone else. Audrey's example points out how difficult it is to know when a relationship is truly over, that breakups often require considerable effort to ensure that they actually occur, and that there are often long periods of uncertainty about whether one is breaking up for good. Disconnecting can take as much work as connecting. People often rely heavily on second-order information, the information that can often seem accidentally revealed, to try and figure out whether it is a breakup or a break.

Fake Statuses

Like Katie in chapter 2 who declared on her Facebook profile that she was in a relationship with a dog, people will often claim joke relationships through their relationship status. This can create an interpretative dilemma: How do you know when to read the relationship status as serious? People will often look for other clues on the Facebook profile. If a man claims to be in a relationship with another man but also claims he is interested in women, the relationship status is probably a joke. The Gunslinger found that he had posted a relationship status that could easily confuse women he was interested in because he was "in a relationship" with a platonic female friend at another college. Gunslinger did this to express his unease with how Facebook seemed such a dominant way to learn information about other people.

> A girl I have gone on a few dates with, who I am going on a date with tonight actually. She had talked to some friends of mine about it after I had asked her out. And she is like: "Isn't he in a relationship?" And they said: "It's apparently not real." So, I mean, I also like the fact that I had it up because I am quite picky. And if she is interested in me enough that she would ask about it, or ask me about it, preferably, then I would tell her. Otherwise, I probably wouldn't be interested in her anyway.

Posting this relationship was part of a screening mechanism for potential girlfriends—he wanted to be involved only with women who thought to ask his friends rather than taking Facebook at (forgive me) face value. Gunslinger was a bit unusual in having a fake straight relationship when he himself was straight. Most straight students I interviewed claimed that joke relationship statuses tended to be with good friends of the same gender. Many women had joke relationship statuses with their best friends from home and often used the relationship status to mark a strong friendship with someone who lived elsewhere.

Joking relationship statuses could cause their own dilemmas when friends had a falling out, or when women wanted to indicate that they were involved with someone new. Do you "break up" with your best friend to let everyone know you have a new boyfriend? Kathleen told me a complicated version of this problem. Her boyfriend, Jonah, decided that he no longer wanted to be Facebook official; he had decided that Facebook was a ridiculous medium to use to announce how committed one felt to another person. Jonah made this decision without consulting Kathleen while they were on a break, but not broken up. In response, she decided to claim to be married to her best friend on Facebook.

> *Kathleen:* And then she just divorced me the other day. It was really rough, and now I am not in any relationship on Facebook.
>
> *Ilana:* Did she let you know that she was going to divorce you on Facebook?
>
> *Kathleen:* She did not. This happened yesterday actually.
>
> *Ilana:* This is terrible timing.
>
> *Kathleen:* No, it was great timing. She had to send a message to *her* boyfriend that she had put a "single" link, so now it says that she is single. Not just married to me, now she is single and completely separate from this other guy.
>
> *Ilana:* So she is breaking up with her boyfriend?

Kathleen: Mmhmm [yes].

Ilana: And what stage is the breaking up that she had to do this?...So she had to divorce you to become single?

Kathleen: Exactly, so that he knew. Not just that she was really good friends with me, but that she was completely single. It's not like anyone really thought we were married or dating or anything. People didn't think that, but she had to make sure.

Ilana: People knew that what you were doing was having her as a placeholder.

Kathleen: Exactly. She was saying "I don't need a crutch." And I needed one. So I was like "Well, fine, good, I don't need you either." So of course I am desperately trying to find someone, and it's just hysterical to try to find someone before someone can notice that I am not married anymore. I know what I am doing in my head, and I know it's childish. But if I don't have someone there, I can't put "single" yet, because Jonah and my relationship isn't right at that "done and completely over" space.

Kathleen understood full well the absurdity of her situation. She wanted to be involved with someone because of the dynamics of her relationship, her best friend wanted to be single because her romantic relationship had changed. Both were using Facebook's relationship status to send second-order information to their boyfriends, but they wanted to send different kinds of information, putting them at cross-purposes. Kathleen was good-natured about her friend's decision, and her friend was lucky. Sometimes "ending" a relationship status link on Facebook between good friends can lead to hurt feelings and conflict when the friend who is "dumped" is not so understanding.

Revealing That You Know

As these new technologies change how second-order information circulates, people are constantly faced with new social dilemmas engendered by how second-order information is now distributed. The previous examples all emphasized interpretive questions people faced: How can one best understand the second-order information that a statement contains in a particular medium? What does that information reveal about someone's intentions and was that an accidental revelation? People I interviewed faced other dilemmas as they tried to figure out when it was appropriate to reveal that they knew something and, often, how to conceal that they wanted to know something as well. I asked Amelie when she revealed in face-to-face conversation that she had gleaned information about people from their Facebook profile. She said that she never did this.

> *Ilana:* So what do you do when you know information about people that you only find out through their Facebook?
>
> *Amelie:* I would never tell them. Actually, I don't know if you would call this stalking, but this girl that actually lives on my floor, she was in a Facebook group sometime before we started, over the summer. And it was a residence group where people who knew they would be living there would join the group, and that was it basically. I would join that group too, and I saw her there, and I noticed that she was living on the same floor as me, so I went to her profile and I sort of checked out what kind of stuff she liked. But when I met her in person, I never told her that. I never told her that I saw her on Facebook, and I know what kind of music she likes, and some of the pictures she has, and yada yada yada.

Amelie spoke to a crucial concern that people had in managing information flow: when and how to reveal information in a different medium than the medium in which one obtained the information. People often develop rules with their friends for when and how to do this, but these rules are not widespread. People are regularly encountering others who do not share these rules. For example,

Anne told me how strange she found it when a woman in one of her classes texted her because she had gotten Anne's phone number from her Facebook profile.

Both Anne and Amelie described inappropriate revelations as "creepy"—an adjective that kept coming up in interviews. College students now will often use *creepy* to describe someone who ineptly manages the information flow and, in particular, the second-order information flow that indicates what one knows and how one knows it. Letting people know that you know something when knowing expresses too much interest in another person's life is creepy. This has been a violation of social expectations long before the technologies I have been discussing were invented. There is nothing new about being creepy. But the term "creepy" is starting to be used more and more frequently for certain kinds of social violations. Any form of claiming inappropriate familiarity can be labeled "creepy"; for example, a man "poking" a woman on Facebook that he doesn't know well enough[5] or texting someone you don't know well because their phone number is available on their Facebook page.

It is also creepy to create a false profile to seek information in a network one doesn't have access to. People are very anxious not to reveal how curious they are to know certain tidbits of information, and they will go to great lengths to conceal their curiosity. It is the *curiosity* that is the second-order information they try so hard to hide. To friend an ex's new girlfriend or boyfriend, for example, is to reveal in a single gesture that you still think about your ex and want to know who they are with now.

5. Facebook gives you the option to "poke" another profile, which creates an announcement on the poked profile "so-and-so has poked you." This has been a feature of Facebook since it began in 2004. There are several different definitions circulating about what it means to "poke" someone.

Facebook Stalking and Other "Creepy" Practices

"Creepy" is not the only term being used more and more frequently nowadays to talk about information flow. College students also talk about "stalking," although it no longer has quite the negative connotation it used to have when referring to physical stalking.

> *Amelie:* I would say that I have a pretty mild definition of it [stalking]. How do I put this? I feel like people use "stalking" lightly now. So when I say I am Facebook stalking somebody, it doesn't mean that I am obsessed with them in the way that real-life stalking is. It just means that I might have checked their profile a few times but I've never met them. Or it means that, um, you know maybe you habitually check somebody's profile that you've never met. Or maybe you met them once and you check their profile all the time. But I think it definitely has to do with not actually telling them that you are checking on them. I think a really defining characteristic is, there is being creepy, which we discussed earlier, which is like the actual interaction without, you know, any real reason. And then there is the stalking, which is you know checking and stuff, but it is just your thing and maybe the other people that you know, know about it, but the person never finds out.

Facebook stalking is intended to be invisible to the person stalked, unlike traditional stalking in which the pursuer wants the other person to know that they are being pursued. In his book on stalking, Bran Nicol writes: "Stalking is an extreme way of reminding its victim that they are in a *relationship* with another person" (Nicol 2006, 30, emphasis in the original). Part of any message the non-Facebook stalker sends contains the second-order information: I can contact you, you are accessible to me, you know that I think of you, I am part of your context. In contrast, Facebook stalkers desperately wish to avoid sending precisely this type of information. Gwen explained:

> *Gwen:* I remember the "Facebook stalk" term—when I was a freshman in college, that was a well-known term. [In one of my classes,] we had to teach a lesson on anything we wanted, so my lesson was Facebook stalking. I actually taught a lesson on Facebook stalk, and how it is so much better than old stalking, where you would follow the person and hide behind places. Now you can do it from a computer, and they have no idea that you are even doing it. So that is how into Facebook I was.
>
> *Ilana:* And what were the other tips?
>
> *Gwen:* There was: Friend their friends and, you know, see what mutual friends you have and see decent photos through their friends. That is always a big thing I tell people because the photos, those will tell you what is going on, or what they want you to think is going on at least.

Facebook stalking came up often in interviews. People told me about checking on their lovers' profiles regularly to see if the Facebook profile might contain traces of other flirtations. They looked at their ex-lovers' profiles to see what was happening in the person's life. They also searched for information on new lovers, or possible lovers, occasionally going to great length to gather information. These searches could take hours in people's days, as they searched through posted photos and people's profiles that were linked to the person they were most interested in. Yet all this labor was done under the assumption that the person being stalked would never know. Interviewees would occasionally talk with horror about Facebook applications that one could choose to add to one's profile that could let people know who looked at their profiles and how often. They admitted that these applications would prevent their stalking. Facebook stalking is something one might confess to one's friends but only rarely (and even then, generally with some shame) to the person or people being stalked.

The impulse to conceal Facebook stalking is so strong that people will go to great lengths to hide how they are exercising their curiosity. To understand the difficulty of ensuring secret Facebook stalking, one needs to understand how Facebook privacy settings function. The person controlling a Facebook profile chooses their level of privacy, which means choosing who else is allowed to view the profile. Some people allow anyone to view their profile; others allow only Facebook friends; and a few restrict various parts of their profiles from specific potential viewers such as their younger siblings and professors. Thus one of the first challenges for a determined Facebook stalker is to circumvent another profile's privacy settings, which often entails becoming someone's Facebook friend. Yet, one often does not want to be the friend of someone one is stalking—friending your ex-boyfriend's new girlfriend lets her know of your unseemly curiosity and continued feelings for your ex-boyfriend. This friend request contains the sort of second-order information Facebook stalkers most earnestly wish to avoid announcing.

There are generally two ways to gain access to someone's profile without revealing one's own desire to gain this access. Both common strategies involve others' assistance; secret stalking is something friends often will help each other to accomplish. First, one uses a friend's profile to see what is posted on a profile only the friend has access to.

> *Anne:* I have done this with my roommate. She will go, "Oh, I am not friends with her." And I will go "Oh I am." And then I will log on. And I will let her look. It's not giving out the password, but it's giving out the information.

In addition, your friend can "friend" the person you want to learn more about without revealing whose curiosity motivates the offer of Facebook friendship. Sometimes people go further and share Facebook passwords with each other so that they can have access to the other person's Facebook network. The second common strategy is to create a fake Facebook profile and use the fake profile to friend people one is curious about.

Fake Facebook profiles can be used to conceal identity not only to hide an embarrassing desire for knowledge but also to conceal who is revealing knowledge. Sometimes college students use fake Facebook profiles to convey information anonymously. Rose told me that in her circle of acquaintances, which involved many athletes, women were often faced with an ethical dilemma. They would know that an acquaintance's boyfriend was cheating, often by finding the evidence on Facebook. They might want to warn the girlfriend, but they wanted to do this anonymously to avoid a public betrayal of their friendship with the boyfriend. As a way out, they would create a fake Facebook profile for an hour or two.

> *Rose:* There is the "create an anonymous Facebook account so you can tell the person [about their boyfriend's cheating] without them knowing you told them." I know people who have done that. You go into Facebook and you create a profile—I am "Sara Smith." And I send a message to this girl saying "Hey, look at this picture under this guy, under this person, and you will see your boyfriend kissing some girl. Just wanted to let you know." Send the message, and then you delete the account. And she finds it, never knowing who told her.

When you want to maintain a fake Facebook profile for longer than a few hours, you have to be careful that all the information you are compiling on the profile is believable. Fake profiles are challenging to do properly. One needs enough friends in one's network to look realistic. One also needs a sense of what this character's consumer taste might be.[6] Sometimes people will create a more realistic fake profile by pooling together their Facebook resources; that is, by sharing a fake Facebook profile. Five to twenty people will have access to this fake profile, using it to gain information by "friending" others without revealing who wants to know the information.[7] And the more friends a profile has, the more realistic it looks.

No matter how much care you take making a fake Facebook profile, you can sometimes slip up with an obvious mistake, like posting an easily findable profile picture. Paul told me about Susie, a female friend who created a male fake Facebook profile to make her boyfriend jealous. He told me about his conversation with another mutual friend, Jessica, about Susie.

> *Paul:* She [Jessica] told me: "I really never believe what Susie says anymore, because she is kind of known as a compulsive liar."
>
> [*Paul*] *Really?*
>
> [*Jessica*]: You know one of her friends on Facebook, Wolf O'Malley?
>
> [*Paul*] *I say:* "Yeah."
>
> [*Jessica*]: Like: "We all think he is fake."
>
> [*Paul*] *Like:* "What? What do you mean?"
>
> [*Jessica*]: "Well, if you look at his friend's list, the only friend he has is Susie.
>
> *Ilana:* Oh, that is a bad fake Facebook profile.

6. In chapter 5, I describe how Kathleen told me in no uncertain terms that no guy acknowledges in their preferences that *The Notebook,* a recent romantic movie, is a favorite film; this was the sign that let her know a particular profile was fake.

7. One woman I interviewed talked about how her group of friends was so aware that this was a problematic practice that their password for their shared fake Facebook profile was "creeper."

Paul: And, when he was created, the day he was created, was around the same time that Seth and Susie had a really big fight. And then if you Google "water polo guys" his picture pops up as one of the first ones.

It wasn't only a profile's photos, number of friends, or likes and dislikes that people had to get right when constructing a fake Facebook profile. Sometimes people had to be careful with the ways in which the technology's interface shaped interactions. Duae Vultae explained all the effort she put into creating a fake instant messaging profile as a practical joke so that she could convince her cousin that a cute Korean guy had fallen for her. She used photographs of a Korean movie star and created a fake IM account to contact her cousin.

Ilana: She must have been very suspicious about this Korean celebrity for a while.

Duae Vultae: I bet she was suspicious. And whenever I felt like she would be suspicious, I would [pause] because I can sign into two accounts at the same time, I tried not to make it so that when I signed on to mine, the other one would sign on too. So there, most people usually check the accounts that are on. If that account is on at the same time and goes off at the same time, they figure it out. So I tried to, you know, log on to different accounts at different times. I guessed that fooled her for a little while. And then I wouldn't talk to her for too long. Usually every chatting session would be at most half an hour. And I usually didn't go on very often, I tell her I'm busy.

Duae Vultae tried to manage all the second-order information that IMing can reveal to make the fake profile as believable as possible. Paying attention to how a medium conveyed information was important, whether stalking, trying to make a boyfriend jealous, or trying to pull off a successful prank.

Second-Order Information and New Relationships

Part of the effort of becoming friends or lovers is learning to interpret the second-order information that accompanies messages whatever the medium. Courtney explained that it took her a while to learn a new person's texting style.

> You know what I find is hard is when you meet a new friend. Because you don't know how they text. And I know when I came to school I found that was weird because you'll be talking to someone, and like I said, I know how my roommate texts, and I know when she puts two *y*'s [e.g., heyy] and when she puts one [e.g., hey], and when you meet a new friend you don't know. So then you don't know—you can't read their texting, which is frustrating because with your actual friends you can read it, like you know exactly how they're feeling through it.

People use second-order information all the time as they decide whether they want to start a relationship, determine whether the other person is interested in a relationship, and struggle to evaluate or respond to a breakup. In part, second-order information seems so confusing and compelling to people in guiding their interpretation of a message because they don't know how intentional the second-order information is.

Second-order information may be the inadvertent tell that points to as-yet-unrevealed feelings, expectations, or contexts. So second-order information may seem more significant than the actual content of a message precisely because the information appears to be transmitted accidentally. For instance, it may be information that people can't help but send with the message because of how the technology is structured (such as the time and date of a message). When a friend starts a text message with "hey" instead of her usual "heyy," is she indirectly letting Courtney know that she is angry with Courtney, or is this just an accidental omission?

> *Courtney:* Because you can read into a text message so much. Like we were talking the other day, and I was telling her how, um, I didn't know if my roommate was mad at me because when she texted me back she only put one "y" with her "hey." And like usually like when we're being friendly we'll be like "heyy" with two "y"s. Or like something like that. And she was saying for her birthday her ex-boyfriend texted her and said "Happy Birthday Lindsay" period, and she knew that he was cutting it short, and she said that was so rude of him, and I said that yes, it was kind of weird. But it was because he put a period. So you can really read a lot into texting. And if you're fighting, and you are mad about something, I know that last night my boyfriend is mad at me about something because I texted "I love you," and he said "You too" not "I love you too." It's just so stupid, but you read into it all. It's like a whole other language in your texts. 'Cause you can't talk about it, like you can't emphasize your points, so you just add extra letters and periods, and they get the point.
>
> *Ilana:* What do you do when this happens, when you get only one *y* in your hey?
>
> *Courtney:* Well, I told my friend, I was like, "I wonder if Joan's mad at me, she just texted me back with only one *y*," and she started laughing at me and she was making fun of me but she understood what I meant. But it sounds stupid when you say it, but she understood. She would think the same thing.

Sometimes the more you know someone, the easier it is for you to interpret their texting styles. Courtney learned to notice an extra *y* in a friend's "hey" or the effort put into texting a full "I love you too." But increased familiarity only helped her notice these patterns. She still didn't know if the omissions were intentional or not. Second-order information was often fascinating for people because it was ambiguous whether it was intentionally transmitted or not. The more you know someone, the more contextual information you might have for deciphering this.

When a woman was deciding whether to get involved with someone, she sometimes paid a lot of attention to the medium used for contact and how frequently messages were exchanged. Women saw the choice of media and the frequency and timing of the messages as indications of not only how serious the man was but also how time intensive any relationship with him might be. Women were often ambivalent about how a serious relationship might affect the time they had to study, earn money, or spend time with friends. This ambivalence could lead them to say "no" to men who seemed like they might want to spend too much time with them, indicated by texting or IMing them too much at the beginning stages of a possible relationship.

Most college students don't think that women might be ambivalent about being in relationships; there is a widely held stereotype that women are always interested in stable and serious romantic relationships. In fact, the stereotype is that women always want to be more committed than men do to a relationship. Obviously this is not always the case. My colleagues Laura Hamilton and Elizabeth Armstrong have discovered that this expectation causes all sorts of dilemmas for women as they make romantic choices in college (Hamilton and Armstrong 2009). Armstrong, Hamilton, and their team of sociologists spent a year living in a freshman dorm at Indiana University. They observed how a floor of women from different social class backgrounds negotiated dating in the first year of college and then interviewed the same women about their experiences for the next four years. They found that college students generally believed all women wanted to be in relationships. Yet the women were often concerned about the social costs of relationships. The committed relationships tended to be very time intensive, which the people I interviewed saw as a change from previous generations' dating expectations. As Audrey explained:

> *Audrey:* [In the past] your lives didn't revolve around them. Now it's to the point that I date a guy on campus, I seriously went over, and we had classes, and then we do homework, and then I spend the night there. Girls literally live there four days out of the week. My roommate has a new boyfriend, and she gets all stressed out because she has stuff to do. But he has to see her after class, and then so she has to move it around. It's like they are all of a sudden something you have to incorporate into your daily schedule. Now they are a two-hour class that you have to incorporate daily into your schedule. But you want to, if you really like the person, you'll do it.

Hamilton and Armstrong found that relationships often took more time than Audrey's suggested daily two hours. Romantic relationships in college often become all-encompassing; people devote so much time to their relationships that they have trouble juggling their other obligations to working, studying, and spending time with friends. Yet there is also enormous social pressure to be in a relationship.

In my interviews, I found that women responded to this dilemma in various ways. Armstrong noticed that women in college sometimes use hookups or casual relationships as a way to avoid the time constraints that seemed to them inherent to being in a relationship. In addition, both Armstrong and I came across many women who were in long-distance relationships, who preferred being involved with someone farther away. This often bought them much-needed time on a daily basis, although some, like Audrey, were ambivalent about being separated for long periods.

> *Audrey:* It makes it a lot easier. I don't know, I guess right now I have met two people, one lives in Chicago and one lives in Detroit.
>
> *Ilana:* There you go—distance.
>
> *Audrey:* Yes, I like distance. I like distance up until a point. My dad says that once I fall, I fall hard. I fall hard and then I want them around all the time. But until then I like distance. And everything is done over the Internet.

Audrey went on to point out that she not only initially preferred long-distance romance but also tended to have long-distance close friends.

> Even with my best guy friends, it's like if you don't want to talk about boyfriend/dating, my best guy friends all go to University of Minnesota and … [w]e probably talk more and have more in-depth conversations while we are away from each other over the Internet then we will actually at home together sometimes. Because you have a more convenient time to do it, because everyone is so busy. Even if everyone wants to go out for dinner, it is a hard task to get twelve people together for dinner.

College students were able to stay in contact as friends or lovers because of cell phones and the Internet, but they were also able to have more control over the amount of time they spent on a day-to-day basis maintaining these ties.

Women also paid attention to the indications early on in a relationship that men might be too demanding of their time—all through second-order information. Sassie explained to me that she had recently refused to go out with Harry because he texted her constantly and kept checking her Facebook but was unable to talk to her in person. She was especially cautious because her previous boyfriend had monitored her Facebook profile, which had sparked several fights about how independent she wanted to be. Sassie described how she began to notice that Harry seemed to have a different understanding than she did about what texting should be used for and when it is appropriate to reveal that you have seen someone's Facebook profile.

Ilana: How do you know he is checking your Facebook?

Sassie: By subtle comments that he makes. And sometimes when a guy will comment on my wall, he will comment right after, such as, for example, one of my guy friends, who is really attractive and I wouldn't mind talking to him, I took him home from a gathering that we had, and he fell on the ice. It was really funny, and so I was laughing at him. And I wrote on his wall: "I hope your butt isn't too sore, blah-blah-blah," totally trying to give him a hard time about it....And then Harry comments on my wall about something, he changed my oil in my car, and he commented about how when I get home, I need to come get him and he will check to see if my oil level is still good enough for the car to run properly....So I don't know, sometimes I used to be so fanatic about my phone. Because I could never let it go unanswered, or let a text message go unanswered. And now, I don't even want to look at my phone because I am afraid it is him. I try to avoid it....If I could set his text messages to a different ring, that would be a good idea. Text messages I see as a simple "Hey, I'm here" or "I saw something funny today, I thought of you", or just little like, notes, I guess; not a way to try and have a conversation. Because if I want to talk to someone, I will call them. Or I will try to say "hey, can you meet me somewhere so we can have a talk?" or something like that.

Sassie wanted to do well in college, and so she wanted control over her time. This meant avoiding potential boyfriends who might constantly demand her attention through her ever-present cell phone and might monitor her interactions with others on

Facebook. Her overly enthusiastic texter was not only letting her know through the sheer frequency of his texting and the timing of his wall posting that he was interested in her, he was also letting her know that he might make balancing studying and romance a bit too challenging.

Changing Technology after a Breakup

Second-order information plays a role in breakups as well as beginnings. People often sent messages to friends and exes about their feelings and intentions implicitly by the ways they changed their technologies. I have mentioned the information (or lack thereof) that a change in one's relationship status on Facebook can imply. This, however, is just the tip of the iceberg. After a breakup, people will remove all traces of their ex from their Facebook profile, deleting photos and wall posts. They will defriend the ex on their Facebook or MySpace, remove them from their IM list of contacts, and delete their ex's phone number from their cell phones. All of these actions are, of course, loaded. To defriend an ex is often interpreted as a hurtful slight, an indication that the person wants to cut off all contact. Anne told me how offended she was when her current boyfriend defriended her after they had broken up (and before they got back together).

> *Ilana:* Have you been defriended?
>
> *Anne:* Yes, my current boyfriend defriended me.
>
> *Ilana:* Oh!
>
> *Anne:* Yeah! To fill you in, I have to make you a tree chart, this is ridiculous. Chronologically, there is my freshman-year boyfriend. Then I dated the boy from New York. And Kyle, my current boyfriend, that has always been all over the place. So I was with the

boy from New York...and so I added Facebook pictures. And Kyle, I guess, still had feelings or whatever, and deleted me.

Ilana: And how did you know that he deleted you?

Anne: Because my roommate and I were both friends with him, and I was on her profile for something, and I saw him in the box of people she is friends with, but it wasn't "friends in common." And I thought: "What the hell, that's weird." So I clicked on it, and I couldn't see his profile. And I was like: "Are you serious? Did you delete me? You deleted me on Facebook!?" I hadn't talked to him in six months, maybe nine months.

And so I sent him a message on Facebook, and an invite saying, "Did you seriously delete me? Like what the hell?"

I called him, and I was like "Dude, did you delete me on Facebook?" And he just started laughing.

And I was like, "No, seriously, did you delete me on Facebook?"

And he's like, "No, it must be something wrong, I don't know what happened. Sometimes it does that."

"Well, then add me. That's stupid, you should add me. I sent you a request." And then he texted me after we got off the phone, and he said: "Okay, you caught me. I deleted you."

And I was like: "What the hell? Why?!? Why would you do that? I haven't done anything to you. I haven't spoken to you or hurt you. What's your problem?"

He's like: "I couldn't see your profile anymore. I just couldn't do it."

Anne believed that defriending was meant to sever all ties and was only justified if she had done something cruel. As she explained: "That's a big step, you know it's like saying I don't care about you, I don't want updates on your life, I don't want to see you anymore, like, you don't do that, that's like cutting somebody out of your life completely." This was Anne's media ideology about what defriending an ex indicates. As discussed earlier, not everyone who defriends on Facebook is also trying to send the additional information that they no longer want to be in any contact with the person they have defriended.

Defriending someone after a breakup can be a very different move for people than deleting their cell phone number from a phone. People typically talk about defriending as a way to express their hurt and anger. Defriending revolves around preventing someone from having access to your information and having contact with you. By contrast, deleting a cell phone number is all about preventing you from having access to them. College students describe removing someone's cell phone number as a way to keep themselves from calling or texting the person.

> *Ilana:* So have you taken anyone's number out of your phone?
>
> *Trill:* Yes, but I have a lot of saved text messages. They will be there. So if I am really, really desperate to call them or text them, I know that I can go look at my saved text messages and they are right there. Or sometimes I—actually, this is so weird—I don't delete them, I just change the name really quickly. And then I won't know what name it is, so I can't look for it. Unless I really really want to take the time to look for it, but there are a lot of numbers so I don't. And then I don't know where the number is, so I can't text them because it is in there, I just don't know where. It works for the most part until I get really desperate, and then I look for it.
>
> *Ilana:* So who do you do this to?
>
> *Trill:* It's mostly guys. If something has happened. Like with George, I wanted to text him, but I couldn't, so I just changed his name. I didn't delete him, I know that. He might be in there again, I don't know. But I know I didn't delete him. It didn't work, because there was a saved text message from him, so it was like, oh well. I usually do it to guys.

In Trill's case, deleting phone numbers is not enough; she knows that she has access through the traces on messages she tends to keep. So she has to change the information (by changing the name in her cell phone) that accompanies the messages. This is not always enough; when she really wants to know a number, she will ask her friends who happen to have the phone number saved on their phones.

While deleting the cell phone number is about controlling one's own impulses to contact one's ex, keeping the phone number can be using the cell phone's potential to alert people to exactly who is calling. Maria told me that she would never remove someone's cell phone number.

> *Ilana:* Have you ever deleted someone's phone number?
>
> *Maria:* No, and I will tell you why: So you know if they call back, you won't pick it up. Although at the same time, I don't pick it up if I don't recognize the number. Even so, if a person who I don't want to talk to calls, I can see "oh, it is that person" and I am definitely not going to pick it up.

Maria here thought about deleting a cell phone number in terms of screening other people, not in terms of managing her own impulses to call. At other moments in the interview, she talked about how she consciously controlled her own impulses to contact people when it would be unwise, and did not want to use her technology as this type of aid.

Other people use their cell phones' signals, and in particular their ringtones, as a reminder that they aren't interested in talking to someone or that they are convinced the person is untrustworthy. Audrey explained the ways she and her roommates use ringtones to indicate how they feel about those they date.

Audrey: Your boyfriend or girlfriend has their own ringtone....You usually delete their number if you broke up. And then their ringtone is gone. Brad's was some song, and then I deleted it. Luckily I didn't give him a good song. I gave him a song that was popular at the time, but it isn't popular anymore. So it wasn't like a classic that I would hate to have to give up. You know, at least it wasn't something really good or something like James Taylor or something like a really romantic song. It was like some stupid top-of-the-chart little love ditty that they had on....I wasn't about to give him a real romantic mushy song....You can tell by the ringtone who it is, so you are like [as though from a roommate], "Brad is calling." [She mimes answering the phone.] "Brad, she's coming."... And then my other roommate's ringtone is "Shot Through the Heart, You Give Love a Bad Name," that's her exes' ringtone. So when her exes call, "Shot Through the Heart, You Give Love a Bad Name" will go off and everyone knows what's next. And we're like, "Ian, Scott, or Patrick, which is it?" And she's like, "oh, its Scott." It's funny, she and Scott have dated off and on, but he had the ex's ringtone because he kind of screwed up in the past.

Ringtones are good examples of how second-order information functions because people can use ringtones to indicate a specific person or a particular category of people without individualizing (e.g., all family members could be given the same ringtone). Debra told me that she had trouble because she hadn't realized that she was using the same ringtones as a warning and an announcement. She assigned her boyfriend a ringtone and then after they broke up, she assigned her next boyfriend the same ringtone. At first, when the phone began to ring, she couldn't tell whether it was her ex or her new boyfriend. When I asked her why she had done this, she shrugged. She said that she thought of that ringtone as the ringtone designated for a boyfriend and hadn't realized how complicated it could be to keep using the same ringtone for multiple people (especially an ex *and* a current boyfriend). The ringtone was supposed to indicate to Debra who was calling, but because she used it to signal a role (a person who is or had been a boy-friend) instead of a person (Tom or Bill), she was not able to use ringtones to code what turned out to be necessary second-order information.

Sometimes after a breakup, people want to avoid second-order information altogether. Some people would not only change the way they used certain technologies but also stop using certain technologies entirely. After Joseph's girlfriend ended the relation-ship, Joseph mourned the relationship by avoiding ways he might encounter traces of her on Facebook. He also stopped instant mes-saging, in part because he associated it so much with her.

> *Joseph:* I avoided her [Facebook] page consciously, more than I thought about going to it, because part of me didn't want to see things in her news feed, or something that somebody wrote on her wall. I guess I consciously avoided it. I thought I would see something pop up on there. Because I guess that is something you can't control.... At the same time, being on it made me a little nervous to see stuff pop up. I guess it still does, but imme-diately after, I tried not to be on it. And I completely dropped in-stant messenger after that happened. I used to talk to her pretty often on it, because if you both have homework or something to do, it's an easy way to still be able to talk to each other. But when that happened, I completely went off. I have been on twice since, and it's been four weeks since that happened.

As people use a wide range of technologies in the beginning and endings of relationships, they have to figure out how different technologies communicate information. They think about not only the actual content of the message, such as "I don't think this is working out," but also what other information the technology can reveal about someone's intentions and the context in which the message was sent (e.g., at a bar, or first thing in the morning). They might think about people's choices of media in terms of the second-order information that a medium transmits along with its message—some media conceal the time and date the message was sent, for example. When someone chooses to send information on their IM away message, are they intending to conceal the time or date, or are they trying to send the message to anyone who contacts them by IM? People interpreting the message sometimes want to figure out what aspects of the medium the sender wanted to use.

In these moments, interpreting a message depends on three intertwined elements: (1) how second-order information encodes the sender's intentions, (2) how it encodes the context of the message, and (3) how it encodes what the sender knows. It isn't only the receiver of a message who is concerned with second-order information. As I discussed, the sender can also be very concerned about what second-order information accompanies their message. And often, when someone is entangled in second-order information questions such as "Do they know I know?" the person can be trying to avoid sending or receiving any message at all.

People's media ideologies guide them in terms of how they will interpret this second-order information, especially how they will use second-order information to try and decipher someone else's intentions. People won't interpret this information in the same way. How they understand the information depends on what they think about the structures of technology, the other media that someone could use to send a message, and what they know or have deduced about the other person's daily life. Remediation, media ideologies, idioms of practice—all play a role in how people use technologies to circulate knowledge and interpret intentions.

5

Breaking Up in a Public

As Frank explained it, it was all Oprah's fault. His parents, strict Baptists, had no idea what he was doing in college. They didn't know he lived with his girlfriend or that he went to quite so many parties. Then Oprah had a show about children's private lives and urged parents to search Google for their children's names. Persuaded by Oprah, his parents quickly found Frank's blog, which he posted under his full name. In his blog, Frank wrote about absolutely everything—he was honest about all his college experiments on his blog.

> *Frank:* Earlier that week, my brother said: "I think Mom and Dad might be reading your blog because they seem to know a lot of what is going on in your life." I am like: "I really hope not, because there is stuff in there about me having sex and stuff. So I would figure, they are straitlaced Baptists, where I am from is about seventy-five minutes away. They would be here in fifty to kill me if they found out. That is what I always thought. So I wrote another entry saying, "Well, I have been outed. I think my parents are reading my blog, so sayonara." That night, an hour after I published that, I got a call from home, and it was my dad, who anytime it's not fun and games, you duck and cover.
>
> He is like: "You're right, we have been reading your blog."

"How long have you guys been reading it for?"

"A couple weeks, and we read the whole thing."

The thing they were upset with the most was how I represented them. And I was just like "my *friends* read this. Twenty-year-olds are reading this. Not like your friends, not other fifty-year-olds." Their justification with this, and I don't know, it is something a logical debate could be held over it, I was saying, "This is private. And it was linked from my Facebook so my peers could read it and not you guys."…They were really upset about how I was representing them, like I said. Their rationale was: "You put this in a public forum, anybody could read it. Why couldn't we?" And I am like: "Because this is something I have had a few nightmares about, you guys reading the private content of my blog." I don't know, it is like the modern equivalent of your parents finding your *Playboy*s under your mattress.

Ilana: It's kind of worse.

Frank: Yeah, like finding condoms in your wallet.

Ilana: Again, I think it's kind of worse.

Frank: Well, it is the modern equivalent.

Ilana: No, it is them reading your diary, this was your diary. But it was a public diary.

Frank: It was public for the five people who read it regularly and commented on it. Yeah, anybody could get to it. But I was banking on the lack of Internet savvy my parents have.

I was a bit surprised that he had posted a public blog with his full name as the blog's title and yet did not expect that his parents would read it eventually. They were most definitely *not* part of his imagined audience. He believed that people would primarily access his blog through his Facebook profile, and so the audience he wrote for was his Facebook network (and his parents weren't on Facebook). It hadn't occurred to him that people, especially the wrong people, might search for his name on the Internet and find his blog that way. We talked a bit about how he could express himself now that he no longer felt safe to write openly on his blog.[1] I thought he could keep a private diary, or send mass e-mails or Facebook messages to his friends. My first suggestion—Why don't you write in a bound journal?—met with puzzlement. Frank pointed out that if he wrote in a journal, his friends couldn't read it. But none of my other solutions addressed the crux of the matter either: Frank wanted to provide regulated, unobserved, and nonintrusive access to his friends who might want to read his blog.

Changing Definitions of Publics

Why were we miscommunicating? I thought people speaking in public contexts such as blogs would value the idea that they were speaking to an anonymous public. From my perspective, *public speech* meant speaking to a crowd of relative strangers; an anonymous audience is an important element of this type of communication. Not so for Frank, and not for many others I have spoken to during this research. Some of the students I interviewed discussed calculating the different levels of accessibility their audience members might have as they typed. They defined the potential audiences for their messages in terms of whom they and the medium might allow to participate. These people liked to imagine that they had control over who might be in their audience; they wanted to control access to their communication, however imperfectly.

Other students, however, were as mystified as I was about what people would say in a public forum. People were developing

1. He has since gone back to blogging his personal life in detail. As of January 28, 2009, three people acknowledge following his blog under his real name.

diverging ideas about what should be said in public and what it meant to be part of a public. Several interviewees mentioned how others on Facebook simply don't understand what it means to put certain kinds of information out there for anyone to see.

This was a dilemma for people at Indiana University and in the United States in general. A year before I began my research, Indiana University plastered the campus with a colorful poster announcing "I Facebooked You," warning students to be careful what they posted on their Facebook profiles in case the wrong person saw it. News stories about new media often revolve around supposedly inappropriate public statements.[2] This was a common anxiety or confusion. People of all generations were concerned about how others were drawing lines between what should be said in public and what should be said in private. In this chapter, I explore the question: Why do many people of all generations believe that bloggers and Facebook users lack common sense or are rude when they post public statements, while as many other users believe this is perfectly acceptable?

Rather than being rude or thoughtless, people are operating according to two different set of principles underpinning what it means to be part of a public when they post. There is a sea change occurring in the United States. Some people (and I am one of them) understand public utterances in terms of anonymity and as communication between assumed strangers. When the person speaking is well known, the author or speaker's anonymity isn't the issue. What makes the public anonymous is that the person is

---

2. An example of this tension is Emily Gould's description of how blogging contributed to a breakup in her article "Exposed" in the *New York Times Sunday Magazine* (Gould 2008) and all the critical comments (see online "Readers' Comments") that her article inspired.

addressing others who are strangers. From this perspective, there are simply some things you don't say in public.

My fieldwork has revealed that this is no longer the issue for other people engaged in public dialogues. These others evaluate the same types of exchanges in terms of accessibility with people to whom they have at least a passing acquaintance. They view most communication as conversations between people who have a regulated range of access to the messages. As Amelie explained in discussing why she would never tell someone that she knew about their musical taste only from reading it on their Facebook profile:

> It's weird, because you make it public. So it shouldn't be all that weird to find out that people see it, but it is. I think when people think of public, they mostly just think of their friends or even their friends' friends. But people don't really realize how public "public" is. So I think that is why it is so weird to find out that a stranger has seen this stuff.

If Amelie is right, then the question people pose when speaking publicly isn't what should or should not be said in a public arena but rather who has access to the communication. Violation of what it means to speak publicly from this perspective is allowing the wrong people—such as parents, employers, police, ex-lovers, and ex-friends—to read or participate in the conversation.

Because of the Internet, and Facebook in particular, break-ups can involve audiences in ways that people are still trying to understand.[3] Facebook allows people to announce their breakups publicly: by changing the relationship status on their profile, announcing it on their status updates or wall posts, or revealing this

---

3. I use *publics* and *audiences* interchangeably in this chapter, although this is too imprecise for scholars who study publics (Barber 2007; Barker 2008; Bauman and Feaster 2005; Gal 2002, 2005; Warner 2002).

in their posted photographs. While blogs and e-mail can also be used to announce breakups publicly, almost all the stories I heard involved Facebook. People talked about how Facebook made them conscious and concerned about public statements in ways that they hadn't been concerned about before. Part of people's relatively new awareness of who has access to public speech acts is the result of how they are interpreting the structures of technologies such as Facebook that allow them to make conscious choices about access. Frank and Amelie are both describing changes in some of the ways that people conceive of publics, public statements, and how to draw the boundaries between what is public and what is private.

People have long understood that speaking to a public meant speaking to a set of indefinite and impersonal others. When someone writes a letter to the editor of a newspaper, the person knows that more people than the editor will read the letter if it is published. The author doesn't, however, know exactly who is going to read the letter. When the author's uncle reads the letter, he will understand that he is part of the intended audience but not the only audience member. His niece could have wanted him to read this letter, but not only him. The author is imagining a range of indefinite readers, and so every sentence can be read as addressing you the reader and an indefinite reader. You are part of the public the text addresses, but you are not the only public (or else you would have gotten the letter sent to you in your mailbox). What is more, the others addressed by this letter to the editor are anonymous. You know there are other readers, but you don't know specifically who they are.

Public Speech

Listeners to public speech also understand themselves to be part of a community of strangers. Public speech is speech that is read or heard by a particular person at the same time that it is read or heard by an indefinite number of impersonal others. This point is crucial for Michael Warner, a social theorist who has written a transformative book, *Publics and Counterpublics* (2002). He argues that public speech is defined by its multiple address—the way it can be interpreted as addressing a person and the group the person belongs to at the same time. "With public speech...we might recognize ourselves as addressees, but it is equally important that we remember that the speech was addressed to indefinite others; that in singling us out, it does so not on the basis of our concrete identity, but by virtue of our participation in the discourse alone, and therefore in common with strangers" (Warner 2002, 77–78). To understand any public speech, according to Warner, one has to keep in mind that it is also always addressed to strangers, that the audience is also always anonymous.[4] To be part of a public, one has to be able to understand this form of anonymity, how people can all be part of an audience of strangers who are bound together, not despite this anonymity but through this particular form of anonymous address. This anonymous address presupposes shared understandings, a shared imagination. Like media ideologies, this imagination of anonymity is neither true nor false. It is simply

4. Warner's emphasis on how public speech always involves an anonymous public has political implications. Warner is developing an insight of Benedict Anderson's in his foundational work, *Imagined Communities* (1999). Anderson asks how, after centuries of identifying as part of an empire or part of a religion, did people start to imagine themselves as being part of a nation? Anderson argues that for nationalism to be compelling to people, it was crucial for people to believe that they were connected to someone they had never met in person because they were both citizens of the same nation. What Warner describes as integral to public speech—that is, this implicit address to strangers—for Anderson is crucial to the rise of nationalism.

an essential element of how one has to interpret public speech in order for such speech to make sense.

What Frank and others like him helped me to realize is that some people no longer presume that public speech involves addressing an anonymous audience. What Warner argues is true of publics in general may in fact be both culturally specific and historically bound. The people I interviewed were moving away from reflexively understanding public speech in terms of anonymous address. Instead, it matters much more to them who has access to certain conversations and speeches, and who reveals they have this access. Audiences may occasionally be anonymous, but this is no longer the only conscious way people are engaging with audiences. Anonymity is no longer central to how everyone hears or evaluates public speech. For some, accessibility has become the self-conscious measure for how to interpret words as public, not anonymity.

This is not to say that everyone nowadays evaluates public speech in terms of accessibility over anonymity. Indeed, I would suggest that what people I interviewed often characterized as a generational or sometimes even technological divide is actually better understood as a difference in imaginations or perspectives. I would interview undergraduates who expressed the same dismay as forty-year-olds might about this newfangled take on what it means to speak in public. Well-known political blogger Arianna Huffington and television comic news anchor Jon Stewart were talking across this divide in a *Daily Show* interview on December 3, 2008. Huffington was promoting her new book on blogging and encouraging Jon Stewart to participate in this form of public communication. Both Huffington and Stewart are part of the same generation, yet in the exchange below, they were talking at cross-purposes, with different understandings of the nature of address at the heart of public speech.

> *Stewart:* When does the need become pathological? You asked me backstage, "When are you going to blog for me?" And I told you, I have a television show.
>
> *Huffington:* I know.
>
> *Stewart:* So when I have thoughts, I put them on the little screen in the living room.
>
> *Huffington:* But I bet you have more thoughts than you use in the show. And I am a blogging evangelist.
>
> *Stewart:* But why should I give people the dreck? Shouldn't I try to focus it and make it as good as I can? Because my other thoughts, there is a reason I haven't put them on the show. No?
>
> *Huffington:* No. You don't understand blogging. You really absolutely have to read the book. Because blogging is not about perfectionism. Blogging is about intimacy, immediacy, transparency, and sharing your thoughts the way you share it with a friend. So anytime you want to blog…
>
> *Stewart:* So it is like intimacy but without having to be in contact.
>
> *Huffington:* Exactly, and also without having to hear your accent. In my case, it is one of the great things about blogging.
>
> *Stewart:* Anonymous intimacy.
>
> *Huffington:* It's not anonymous. Your thoughts are very much your own, very personal…

When Huffington rejects the idea that blogging is anonymous, she responds as though Stewart was suggesting that he would be an anonymous author, not that he will be addressing unknown people. Stewart, however, describes his possible blogging, and indeed all public speech, as addressing an anonymous audience.

He realizes that public speakers create a public persona; on his show he is performing as the character Jon Stewart, a character that is distinct from who he is at home or with his friends. For him, public speech is most definitely *not* speech to friends. So when Huffington urges him to blog as though he is addressing his friends, he points out the irony in this suggestion from his perspective: this presupposes anonymous intimacy, and hence not intimacy at all. Stewart insists he has a forum for public speech, and it is a forum that requires him to speak with care. Why does he need another forum? Huffington argues that he should explore a forum that not only encourages different kinds of access but also imagines different forms of access for particular media. She imagines that she is blogging to people who fall somewhere on a continuum of access to her words and life (just as Frank does in my opening anecdote). Huffington is addressing her imagined friends and neighbors; Stewart is addressing strangers.

What changes when people start focusing on an audience's access to words instead of an audience's anonymity when thinking about speech as public? When people focus on accessibility, they are much more conscious of who has access to their communications and who does not. Access can still be an issue for people imagining publics as anonymous individuals—some people don't have the money or education to join certain public dialogues. For example, let's say that 40 percent of people in a certain country are illiterate; letters to the editor there would potentially address only the 60 percent of the nation who reads and those who are read to. Yet these are implicit exclusions. Illiterate people are not openly told, "You are not one of the people I address when I write a letter to the nation's reading public." Indeed, to exclude others openly can undercut the ways in which the public is composed of supposed strangers by naming those addressed and those not addressed. In short, when people are thinking about publics as anonymous, access may still be relevant, but it is not often openly discussed or negotiated.

The new technologies people use to address publics often explicitly limit one's audiences. When Facebook first started in 2004, only college students could join. All the undergraduates I interviewed remembered that Facebook used to be limited to college students. They shared this sense that Facebook was originally an age-specific social networking site that marked a certain maturity as well as unsupervised communication. Mary Anne told me jokingly how privileged she was among her group of friends because Indiana University (IU) gave out e-mail addresses (and hence the ability to join Facebook) to high school seniors who had decided to go to IU.

> *Mary Anne:* This was back in the day when Facebook was only for college students. But I, thanks to Indiana University, was the lone high schooler on Facebook, because I had an Indiana e-mail "edu."
>
> *Ilana:* How did you get that?
>
> *Mary Anne:* Because I was accepted at IU, they gave you everything. So I had a Facebook profile. So actually if you go to my Facebook and you look at my first wall posts, actually everyone is like, "You're in high school! Why are you on Facebook? You are too young to be on Facebook!" But I was like "I'm really cool! I have Facebook!" And I would go to school and I'd be like, "I have Facebook and you don't." This was probably December of my senior year, and no one got it until that summer....When I first started on Facebook, it was only for college students, so I was really cool. I was really elite.

When Facebook began to allow high school students to join, Facebook became less a marker of status, although danah boyd

(2007a) suggests it shifted into a marker of being college-oriented. Boyd suggests that MySpace was the networking site for middle school students and high school students who did not actively plan to go to college. Then, in fall 2006, Facebook became available to anyone who wanted to join. Suddenly college students were faced with having parents and potential employers looking at their Facebook profiles. Concern over who had access to Facebook information expanded from careful attention to how one's friends gossiped to concern over how those in authority might monitor.

College students often mentioned their unease that their parents and their friends' parents were now on Facebook and requesting to be Facebook friends. When Facebook introduced privacy settings, this helped quiet their anxieties—Facebook now allows people to control how much one can see on a profile. Yet students still found the fact that "adults" were on Facebook disconcerting; they wanted it to be a space reserved for college students. Lacey told me that she refused to accept a high school classmate's mother as a friend despite repeated requests.

> *Lacey:* When I was coming to school, it was only available to college students, which seemed really normal to me. And now there are people's moms on Facebook, and I am really uncomfortable with that. This girl I was just telling you about [that I used to be friends with], her mom friended me like four times. And every time I was like "NO!"
>
> *Ilana:* Wait a minute. But you aren't friends with her [the girl] anymore.
>
> *Lacey:* I'm not friends with her in real life. I am friends with her in Facebook life. We are friends online.…I am not friends with this girl anymore at all. We never talk or anything, but we are still friends on Facebook. And so when her mom friended me, I was like, "This is too weird."

For Lacey, and others, accepting someone as a Facebook friend was consciously choosing whom she would allow into her Facebook public. She was willing to allow former friends to remain in her public, and she was willing to friend almost anyone she met at IU, but she drew the line at the parent of a high school friend with whom she had had a falling out.

Some college students told me that they did not have a choice about accepting some authority figures as Facebook friends. Mary Anne explained that she worked over the summer as a camp counselor for a religious summer camp and was obliged to accept a friend request from the camp leader.

> *Mary Anne:* The religious leader who runs the summer camp friends all of us. And so he monitors our Facebook. So my Facebook is clean of everything. Even if I am not drinking in a picture, if there is a pitcher of Miller Lite or something in the background, I can't have it on my Facebook. Jason, my boyfriend, had a bunch of beer pong games and everything, you know those applications? He had all those up because he is a basketball player. They were all playing them together. And he actually got a Facebook message that was asking him to please take them off or his employment would be in contention.
>
> *Ilana:* Over an application?
>
> *Mary Anne:* Uh huh, because it is not portraying the [right] demeanor. They [employers at the camp] will look at our wall-to-walls.

Mary Anne became very attentive to what she and others added to her Facebook profile. The price of her steady summer job was a monitored Facebook profile.

Students sometimes found ways around this threatened monitoring. One senior explained to me that she had realized that potential employers might want to see her Facebook profile when they were deciding whom to hire. She created two Facebook profiles: a clean profile under her own name and the "real" profile under a fake name that her friends connected to. Other people simply deactivated their Facebook accounts. Especially if they were athletes, they did not want the hassle or risk involved in having a site public enough that police or coaches would find evidence of underage drinking or other forbidden behavior. Some interviewees became concerned about who had access to their profiles and so created fake Facebook profiles or stopped using Facebook.

In 2007, Facebook allowed people to choose how accessible their Facebook profiles would be to others. One can choose to allow (in order of increasing privacy) (1) anyone on Facebook to see one's profile, (2) only friends and people in one's Facebook "networks" (e.g., at IU that would include anyone with an Indiana University e-mail account), (3) friends of friends (i.e., Facebook friends and any of their Facebook friends); or (4) only Facebook friends (i.e., people one has individually confirmed as a "friend" through one's Facebook profile). Facebook has since added other ways of controlling access to various parts of one's profile; for example, you can now customize, you can choose among the same privacy options to determine who can see photos or who can read your wall. In managing these privacy settings, people are thus managing the publics that their profile addresses. Lisa explained that she had created a fake Facebook profile simply to experiment with how different privacy settings limited others' access to her profile.

> I had two bogus accounts, mainly because I play around with my limited profile a lot. I have three different views of my profile: mine, my friends, and the limited one. And I always want to know what the limited one looks like. And then I opened up another one that I wasn't friends with so I could see what the world saw.

Lisa was aware enough of how Facebook's interface allowed for different types of access that she wanted a mechanism—the fake profile linked to her Facebook profile—to experiment with access.[5]

The Pressure to be in a Facebook Public

Focusing on accessibility when thinking about public statements encourages people to consciously monitor and manage who is part of a public. The examples I have given are all about drawing boundaries, about excluding or wanting to exclude certain people. But when the focus is on access, the converse is also true: When people refuse to join Facebook, this isn't always acceptable for their circle of friends or family. There is considerable social pressure for people to participate in certain publics. People will sometimes create Facebook profiles for others who are reluctant or just can't be bothered. This was especially true for lovers who wanted to make their romantic relationship Facebook official, and hence public, but were thwarted because their lover wasn't on Facebook. If your lover does not have a Facebook profile, you cannot link your profile to theirs through the relationship status feature. You can declare you are in a relationship but not with whom. Some people found it frustrating when others did not reveal who they were involved with. Frank explained that he couldn't see on Facebook who his best friend was dating:

> He is in an open relationship, but his boyfriend does not have a Facebook account, so it just says "in an open relationship." And

5. Lisa did this before the summer of 2008, when Facebook designers changed the interface to allow users to view how various others see their profiles without having to create a fake profile.

that's it. That's the strange thing, to list yourself in a relationship when you don't have a face and a name to go with it. I think it's almost like, I don't know, it's kind of strange. You don't get to see who that person's better half is, and you would kind of learn something about who the person is by who they are dating.

Karen told me that she found out a man she was beginning to date, Aaron, had a profile on Facebook configured by his exgirlfriend. After Aaron asked her out, she checked out his Facebook profile. She was surprised to see that he was "in a relationship" with someone else; asking her out seemed to be cheating on his girlfriend. She decided to go on the date but confronted him right away, telling him that she knew he had a girlfriend because of his Facebook profile. He was confused—he didn't have a Facebook profile. He insisted that his ex-girlfriend must have made it for him without his knowledge. When she told me this, I told her that this sounded like a lie. Karen said that she thought he was lying at first, too, but when she looked more closely at Aaron's supposed profile, she realized that it was a bit too romantic and the posted tastes were suspiciously not the taste of a nineteen-year-old man. What clinched it for her was that he listed *The Notebook* as his favorite movie. No guy, Karen assured me, lists *The Notebook*—the year's quintessential chick film—as his favorite movie. Karen was convinced that this was a fake profile—after all, Aaron didn't even know this profile existed. His ex-girlfriend may have disagreed that it was fake; she could have seen the profile as a necessary component to having a publicly declared and publicly performed relationship.

Not everyone created "fake" profiles for others to see as a way of marking romantic involvements publicly. Lisa, whom I mentioned earlier, created a fake profile so that she could have a friend from Montana—a place she remembered fondly—represented on her Facebook profile.

The reason why I initially did my first fake one is because after I graduated college, I spent some time in Montana. And I really identified with that time in my life. But I feel like people don't see that as much as they do my time in Indiana. And all my friends in Montana, they don't choose Montana as their network. So it is not under my list of networks. I needed one more friend from Montana [so that Montana could be a listed network on her profile]. So that's why I created this.... So I had this fake person that I am starting to personify in a scary way, I think. But I will have him say things to me that I want other people to see like: "How's Josh doing with XYZ?" Because I don't necessarily need to tell the world, "Oh, we're going to Seattle." But I will have this fake person say: "Have a great time in Seattle." So people will see (a) I have a friend in Montana because the network is clearly there and (b) they'll know that we are leaving on a trip without my having to tell them that.

Lisa also used this profile as a quick and convenient way to post information on her profile she wanted others in her Facebook network to know. For knowledge to circulate publicly in the ways some people wanted, belonging to or participating in a public is essential. Sometimes people would create participation for others, real or imagined.

Other people's reluctance or previous reluctance to participate in a Facebook network could create social dilemmas for those in their social circle. Doyle mentioned that he didn't know whether to friend Nat or not. He knew Nat because Nat had dated Jessica, a good friend of Doyle's. Nat had refused to be on Facebook the entire time he was dating Doyle's friend. Now that he was dating someone else, he joined Facebook and was openly involved with his new girlfriend on Facebook.

> *Doyle:* Recently two of my good friends broke up.
> *Ilana:* Did you find out by Facebook?

Doyle: Yeah, no, well, I think that the guy didn't have a Facebook account....He went to Purdue last year, he just transferred to IU this year, never had a Facebook. He just didn't like it, he thought it was evil—I don't know what he thought. He just didn't want to have one. He had one for a day and then deleted it....So her profile said "relationship"—it went from "in a relationship" to, like, nothing. I was just like: "hmmm." And then I had breakfast with her over Christmas break, and she told me about it. I had kind of assumed that that was what had happened, and that was what had happened. But then, afterwards, just a couple of weeks ago, the guy, Nat, gets a Facebook account. And he is living down here now with some other girl that has moved in with him. Now he is in a relationship with her on Facebook. So when you are dealing with this, you don't want to have wall posts from both of them, because both of them are going to be like "What are you saying about me to her?" I was like, "If I add him as a friend, Jessica is going to get mad." He wasn't on Facebook all this time, and then this other girl shows up and gets him on Facebook and is in a relationship with her and all this other stuff.

For Doyle, the aftermath of another person's breakup and subsequent decision to create a Facebook profile had presented him with a quandary of inclusion. Would adding Nat to his Facebook audience be a betrayal of his friend Jessica, Nat's ex?

Multiple Publics

Navigating the fact that certain people have access to one's public utterances can create more social dilemmas than the mere fact of access. One is also faced with the quandary of how to manage one's public performances of friendships, romances, and identity when different audiences can have contradictory demands. For college students, these problems can revolve around having a profile that your family and your friends (or your friends and your lover) all have access to. You may want your profile to anticipate an audience of your parents (or siblings who are likely to tell your parents) differently than a profile would anticipate your friends' gaze. When one thinks of publics in terms of access, one becomes more aware of the multiple audiences that can have access to your conversations.[6]

The Demands of Multiple Audiences

People often experienced this as a dilemma when these multiple audiences made conflicting demands they had to assuage. Some men told me how complicated they found it to have a profile that both friends and girlfriends had access to. A girlfriend might post romantic statements on his Facebook wall that he was too embarrassed to have his friends see. Does he hurt his girlfriend's feelings by deleting the public posts or leave them up and risk his friends' teasing? Facebook profiles allowed for multiple audiences—friends who expected the man to be sociable (showing up in pictures of parties) and a girlfriend along with her friends who expected the man to be faithful (never flirting with attractive women at parties). Photos too could be a problem, revealing that attractive women were at a party but not the actual conversations, flirtatious or not, that the boyfriend had with these women. When the photos were posted and tagged with his name the next day, should he remove his name from the photos? Some men felt caught between the demands of two different audiences for their profile.

> *Alan:* Facebook poses you with [dilemmas]…It's like those books you read which say "go to p. 58 and do this or go to p. 100 and have a completely different story."

6. Facebook in 2009 has begun to address this in its interface.

> *Ilana:* So Facebook is the Choose Your Own Adventure story of romantic fights.
>
> *Alan:* Because there are so many different ways you could go with it.

Alan was starting to feel beaten down by Facebook. Having a girlfriend-friendly profile did not seem possible if he also wanted to attend casual parties that showed up on Facebook the next day.

I interviewed Gwen, who explained what it is like to have access to one's boyfriend's profile when the boyfriend privileges his friends' gaze over hers:

> *Gwen:* I feel like I can't decide whether it is the fact that I checked Facebook that triggered my distrust or that it was I already didn't trust him, and Facebook kind of perpetuated it. We really didn't have issues until I started seeing things on Facebook, like photos—I should probably ask him about this. And every time something new came up, it just got worse and worse. And most of my arguments with him about something that he did, I would not have even known about had I not been on Facebook. I would have been completely oblivious, it wasn't things that I should know, it just didn't matter. Yes, pretty much Facebook perpetuated our arguments on my side.
>
> *Ilana:* He knows that you check Facebook compulsively. You become a major part of his audience when he is managing his Facebook profile.
>
> *Gwen:* Yes, he is doing it with me in mind.
>
> *Ilana:* He knows that there are going to be consequences. He may not be doing it with only you in mind, there may be other people.
>
> *Gwen:* But he knows I'll see it, for sure. Which kind of adds to the whole thing. That's why I felt I should always approach him, that was one of the reasons. Because he does know that I am going to see it. And there were times that he even called me ahead of time

before I had seen it to warn me that something was going to be on Facebook that I would be upset about. Like when a girl sat on his lap, he called me to tell me: "Just so you know, a girl sat on my lap, a picture was taken, it will probably end up on Facebook. I didn't want you to worry about it." So he did know, he obviously knew that I was going to see things like that.

It is partially the public nature of this information that is troubling. Gwen was becoming a witness because she was part of her boyfriend's public, but not the most important part of his public. Since this interview, she has decided not to be Facebook friends with her subsequent boyfriends. By refusing to join her boyfriend's Facebook public, she manages not to become so suspicious.

After the Breakup

During a relationship, people struggle to balance the demands of having a Facebook profile for friends and a lover. Yet in the aftermath of a breakup, people often start anticipating *only* their ex's gaze on their profiles.

> *Kathy:* Moments after I broke up with him, my ex's status read "Ronnie is happy."…I couldn't believe that he had the nerve to pronounce to the world how thrilled he was, so I naturally had to retaliate with "Kathy is having a great day!" or something like that. I am trying to be the more mature one here, but Facebook sure makes it difficult. The worst part is having to make all my statuses so darn happy. Even though I'm glad this is over, I'm still a little sad, you know? Hurt…angry…the typical post-breakup emotions. But instead of saying "Kathy is sad and hurt and sick of assholes," I have to be all, "Kathy can't wait for the weekend!" or some lie like that because he's probably looking. And he probably wants me to be sad and hurt and angry and he probably wants to take great satisfaction in knowing that he's the one who

caused all that. And I absolutely refuse to give him that satisfaction. The next part of my master Facebook plan is to have friends take a ton of pictures of me this weekend looking like I'm having an absolutely wonderful time doing whatever we're doing. Then I'll make a new album with some random name that implies an inside joke he isn't part of, and it'll be great except for the fact that I'll probably still feel like crap. However, my Facebook page will portray me as a bundle of happiness and joy, and that is all that matters.

Kathy and many other women told me about changing their profile to show how happy and carefree they were after a breakup. They would go out immediately after the breakup and have photos taken of themselves with friends, especially male friends. They would ask their male friends to write innuendoes on their Facebook wall and try to use their Facebook profile to inspire jealousy in their ex-boyfriends. While most women talked about performing a false relief on Facebook after a breakup, some talked about expressing their sorrow and rage.

What I found interesting is that post-breakup, the fact that there are multiple audiences for a Facebook profile seems to fade away from these brokenhearted women's consciousness, and they use their profiles solely to send a message to their ex. What I also found surprising was the widespread assumption that after a breakup, an ex-lover could be counted on to check one's profile. I was skeptical, but women I interviewed were confident that the ex always looked.

Audiences' New Obligations

People also regularly dealt with the demands of multiple audiences by actively ignoring one possible audience. In my opening anecdote, Frank wrote a blog for years with the tacit assumption that his parents would never be part of the blog's public. Others, too, reported using this tactic, telling stories like Frank's in which the crux of the story revolves around the revelation that a particular person had unexpected and undesirable access to one's public utterances. For people expecting their publics to be anonymous, this would not be a surprise or a revelation. While people believe that anyone could potentially be in a public when they understand the public to be anonymous, by contrast, people believe that not everyone could potentially be in a public when concerns over access reign supreme.

Being conscious of who has access to a public changes the ways in which multiple publics can be an issue. Multiple publics also accompany public utterances that anticipate anonymous publics. But these multiple publics create different quandaries when people focus on anonymity as opposed to accessibility. Under anonymity, all audiences are imagined to be relatively equivalent. A statement addressing an anonymous city is not significantly different than a statement addressing a nation of strangers, or for that matter a campus of strangers. When you find out your parents are unexpectedly in the public you are addressing, if this is a violation, it is because having parents in your audience is inappropriately mixing the public and the private. Intimate family relations are not supposed to become an issue in an anonymous public. But in a context in which issues of access dominate, the presence of parents is a different kind of violation—people are revealing that they have an unwelcome access to your public words. In this sense, what it means to be public is changing.

This focus on access has led to a new rule of etiquette on Facebook that I, constantly thinking in terms of anonymity, initially found perplexing. Two college women told me that while they read conversations that span two people's Facebook walls (wall-to-wall conversations), they would never admit to doing so. They thought they were being "creepy" when reading because they were violating the profile owner's tacit expectations. I was very confused, and I pointed out that Facebook walls are public. If they had wanted to have a private conversation, the people could send private Facebook messages to each other instead. The women disagreed, arguing that the authors of these texts were not anticipating multiple audiences when they wrote; they were not imagining these conversations as public. When access becomes the issue, people with access can have a new set of obligations—to behave responsibly with the access that they do have, especially since this access may be accidentally or unwittingly given.

This is but one of the ways in which the obligations of being an audience member are beginning to change. Anonymous public members weren't necessarily expected to respond, although they could. But when you know that people have access to certain personal information because they reveal that they engage with your public statements (perhaps by being your Facebook friend), they can feel obligated to respond to certain announcements. What do you do when you find out by Facebook that a friend has just broken up? Do you write them publicly (on their wall), do you call them on their cell phone, do you mention it if you happen to see them in person that week, or simply ignore the information entirely? People who announce their breakups on Facebook are aware that this will trigger a wide range of responses, some welcome and some unwelcome. Rachel talked about the responses she was getting after a recent, painful breakup.

Ilana: Have people been posting on your wall?

Rachel: I have gotten a lot of messages, and a lot of Facebook posts, and a lot of text messages, and a lot of IMs and phone calls. It's

nice because there are people coming out of the woodwork saying, "hey, let's hang out." When I took my relationship status
off, I put [on her Facebook profile] "I don't want to f—ing talk
about it. Don't f—ing ask me." So I get a lot of "hey, I was just
thinking of you." And I am like "yeah, I'm sure. Four of you just
so happened to be thinking of me today, right now. I'm sure."
I got messages from people who were like, "I know you really
don't want to talk about it, but you know, if you want to talk."
Of course, it was my one friend who just got out of a four-year
relationship. And another friend of mine who has been horribly
broken up with by my brother four times. They were on and off
dating for four years. So we're really close. So it was those people,
so it was all right. And then I got some people, I was so mad,
like my best friend from eighth grade: "heyyy, how are you??"
Some girl I took a class with last year who I haven't talk to in
nine months: "Heyyy, whassup?"

Rachel was explaining the wide range of people in her Facebook
network that suddenly had access to information about the fact
that she had broken up but little idea of the details behind the
breakup. Intriguingly, Rachel allowed the news of the breakup to
enter people's news feeds at the same time that she announced that
this was the only information about the event she was willing to
circulate. People contacted her out of curiosity and sometimes they
felt obligated to respond to this information, although, as Rachel
pointed out, they don't always finesse the initial contact as grace-
fully as they could.

Announcements of breakups often seem to require a response,
and some people who use social networking sites are beginning
to interpret intimacy in terms of how responsive and attentive an
audience member is to their profile. Lisa talked about June, whom
she had met only once in person, but she maintained long-lasting
conversations through June's MySpace page.

Lisa: In MySpace, I have a friend who, if she is in a breakup stage or anything bad is going on in her life, everything changes in her background, it suddenly becomes very sad. The colors are dark and somber, the pictures are of roses in the rain, very sad. If she is happy, the colors are brighter and cheery, the fonts are more peppy. And she once said that she once posted to people, "Don't ask me how I am doing, you can tell how I am doing by looking at my profile."…She puts a blog up, tells a story, she changes the actual aesthetics of her profile, and it is all out there for us to observe and study, I guess. So I guess she feels offended when people say, "Oh, how are you doing?" She wants people to actually comment concretely "I am so sorry this happened. But do you want to talk to me about this breakup?" This is actually someone I know exclusively through my boyfriend. I don't know her very well. She is dating one of his good friends right now. And we ended up connecting through MySpace because of that. So she is one of my friends [on MySpace].…

Ilana: Do you let her know that you know, that you have checked her MySpace [profile]?

Lisa: I do with her, she has kind of reached out to me. It's kind of interesting because we met each other once when I went to visit. They live in San Francisco. So I met her one time, and we became friends on MySpace. And that's actually how our friendship grew. I am number 2 on her Top Friends.[7] And I have been for over a year now.

Ilana: So what do you do to maintain number 2?

Lisa: I don't know honestly. It kind of happened. I don't know if maybe it's what I don't do? Because I don't cut ties with her. Because I was number 3 for a while. And the girl in number 2, that's how I knew they weren't friends anymore by the way. They

---

7. Top Friends allows one to list one's top eight friends on MySpace. This was an option originally available only on MySpace although there is now a Facebook application that allows one to list ten top friends.

stopped all their communication on MySpace. And I thought, "She's not on her friend list anymore. They must not be friends anymore."

Ilana: But you comment when the roses in the rain show up?

Lisa: Yes, I know now to go to her blog and comment, "Oh, I'm really sorry that happened, gosh. That sounds rough." I give her my thoughts and my support.

Ilana: And that gets you number 2?

Lisa: Yes!

Ilana: Because you are the right kind of MySpace responder to her?

Lisa: I think so. I actually don't know why I am number 2. I do wonder why. Oh, I should say that I am actually number 3 now because she has a special spot reserved for the person she is dating. And then there is this other girl, that she actually is good friends with, got that spot on MySpace. But I am still there, in front of all these other people who live in San Francisco with her. I haven't really figured out this thing. Because I feel like communication through MySpace in a sense isn't real. It's like a pen-pal relationship. Because she did ask me to be her bridesmaid in the wedding, which shocked a lot of my friends.

Lisa's friends, the ones that she saw in person regularly, were perplexed that June wanted Lisa to be her bridesmaid. This seemed, to them, to be claiming too strong a connection. June was rewarding someone who had proved to be an exemplary member of her MySpace profile's public. Lisa had spent time learning to interpret June's profile and could tell how June was feeling without asking. She had proved herself to be responsible and caring in the way that June wanted from her MySpace public. This MySpace care eventually translated into a role in her in-person wedding. In general, one of the changes from anonymity to accessibility is in people's expectation of audience members. What it means to be an anonymous member of a public is different than being included in a public where everyone is conscious of accessibility.

The Intimacy of Shared Passwords

As ideas about public utterances change, ideas about private utterances and what it means to have access to certain conversations marked as private change as well. One of the new ways the structures of Facebook, e-mail, and other technologies allow people to express intimacy and trust is by sharing passwords. Even someone who reacted with horror at the idea of sharing passwords described it as "a level of intimacy that's just hard to imagine." Exchanging passwords gives lovers and friends access to how someone communicates with others. If publics are now sometimes understood in terms of who has access to particular exchanges and who openly acknowledges these exchanges, privacy is also marked by a form of access—in this case, access to the behind-the-scenes exchanges others can't see.

The stories I heard about exchanging passwords or reading cell-phone messages often had undertones of control and suspicion. This access to all of someone's recorded communication through their cell phone was often a way to gauge how faithful a lover was. Courtney talked about how common it was for people to read each others' text messages.

> *Courtney:* I don't know anyone's boyfriend who does not read their girlfriend's saved texts. The inbox, the outbox, all of them. I know that my boyfriend right now does, as soon as I leave. He won't do this in front of me, he has too much pride. I know that as soon as I walk out the room, he picks up my phone and goes through it.

Ilana: Do girls do this also?

Courtney: Yeah, they do. I guess it goes both ways. But that causes a ton of problems. Things are taken the wrong way.…

Ilana: So do people say, "No, I won't give you my password?"

Courtney: Some people do. My friend from back home, who I was saying knows his girlfriend's passwords, he knows her instant messenger password, her Facebook password, he knows all of that but he will not give her his. He has a lock on his phone where he has to enter the password before you can get on his phone.

Ilana: Wait, so he thinks it is okay for him to have all his girlfriend's passwords, but—

Courtney: He doesn't give her his.

Ilana: Does she say anything about this?

Courtney: No, she doesn't. And me and my boyfriend will always talk about that, because we are all a group of friends, and she won't say anything to him. He'll be like: "Give me your phone." And she will just hand it over. If she is texting, he will come right over and say, "Who are you texting? Why are you texting them?" And he'll get real mad about it. She will say, "Well, let me see your phone." And he will be like, "No!"

Students are uncomfortable about what happens when this new form of intimacy isn't reciprocated—when one member of the couple demands access but won't allow access to his or her own cell phone and accounts. According to Courtney, people were ambivalent about this new form of intimate sharing in general when it was one-sided. In addition, neither she nor her boyfriend will search each other's cell phones openly, but given an opportunity, they will investigate the histories of communications left on each other's phones.

Sharing passwords might be common, but it often seemed to occur as part of an attempt to end a fight. People tended to find the idea of sharing passwords fraught, and they were not always convinced by arguments that sharing passwords was an appropriate way to reveal trust and intimacy. Halle told me about the pressure a former boyfriend exerted to get her to share her password, pressure that she resisted because she didn't accept his claims that this was an issue of trust or intimacy.

> *Halle:* One day we decided we wanted to do the ushering thing at the IU auditorium. And apparently lots of people try to do it. There is a time when you sign in online, and he was going to be in class.
>
> So he was like "I am just going to give you my IU password, sign in and sign me up to usher."
>
> *So I said:* "Okay, that's fine." So I did, and it was fine. So that is where the password thing started.
>
> *Ilana:* Okay. But you had his password, he didn't have yours.
>
> *Halle:* Right. It's a very complicated story. So, I did that, and that was fine. And then a couple of days later, he was in his room with a girl who we had discussed before because she was one of the ones that he really liked to flirt with.
>
> And I said, "Hey, for the past two weeks or so, every time I come over to your room, this chick is already here. You need to chill out a little. Because it is just the two of you. You need to chill out a little."
>
> Because I am not the type of person to kind of sit there and mull things over in my head and not say something. I will say something, because what's the point? Nothing is going to change if you don't say something. So I said something.
>
> And he got so defensive and blew up. "I've never given you any reason not to trust me. Why won't you trust me? That's ridiculous. Blahblahblah."
>
> And then he said, "I even gave you *my password.*"
>
> And I was like: "What does that have to do with anything?"
>
> And then he goes: "Well, you haven't given me yours."

"What??" I said, "Well, why would I? You wanted me to do something for you. Why would I give you my password?"

"Well, because you have mine."

"But that doesn't make sense to me. You wanted me to do something, you don't need my password."

Ilana: And he could have changed it.

Halle: Right, he's not the brightest bulb. We had a big fight about it, because we were both sticking to it out of principle. "No, I'm not going to give it to you." "Well, you should, because you should trust me."

For Halle, this was the beginning of a series of fights that eventually ended in a breakup. Halle and her now ex had very different perspectives on why someone should share a password. Halle saw this as something you do if sharing will help you accomplish a task; her boyfriend saw this as a gesture of intimacy. When other people found themselves caught in a similar cycle of fighting with their boyfriend or girlfriend, they might find the fights too frustrating to keep standing on principle. They would then exchange passwords in the heat of an argument, as concrete proof that they weren't flirting with anyone else. Sharing passwords is becoming a marker of trust and of intimacy, but not uniformly accepted. Some people would tell me that this was something that they did when they were younger, and had learned that they shouldn't. In general, sharing passwords was a double-edged sword for people, opening up the possibilities that their lovers would monitor their conversations and interactions. Trust has become intertwined with issues of privacy in new ways because of the social structure of technology.

PEOPLE are moving from thinking about public statements as anonymous to accessible. Not everyone is changing their understandings of public statements; some people still have a perspective on publics as composed of anonymous strangers, while others now see publics as defined by varying degrees of accessibility. People are often confused that others think about what it means to be public so differently. They are encountering others who understand what it means to speak publicly, to hear or read public texts, and to have private communication all very differently. In this chapter, I considered five central aspects for publics based on accessibility that do not hold for publics that presume anonymity. First, when thinking about publics in terms of accessibility, people no longer assume that anyone, even their enemies or relatives, could potentially be part of their audience. They believe that they have some control over who has access to their words, and that some people can be actively excluded. Second, having the technology or virtual presence becomes essential for participating socially. For example, some people will create Facebook profiles for their lovers so that they can interact as a couple for a Facebook public. Third, when people are conscious that access is a key component in how publics operate, they also become aware that they are sometimes speaking to multiple audiences at the same time. People sometimes face real quandaries determining whether their Facebook profile is addressing their friends, their girlfriend or boyfriend, or their future employer. Fourth, what it means to behave properly as an audience member changes. You have different obligations or expectations as an anonymous member of a public than you do as a member who has access to a public conversation. Fifth and finally, as people's ideas about what it means to be part of a public change, their ideas about the divide between what is public and what is private also changes. In particular, passwords, previously markers of privacy, are now becoming markers of intimacy. Being part of a public is changing because of the ways that people's understandings about what it means to participate in a public are changing.

Conclusion

Lacey wanted to tell a story about fake Facebook profiles in class. But first, she had to explain something. "I like to moon people," she said, "I think it's really funny to moon people." When she said this, all I could think was that, yet again, teaching had started to resemble riding a bucking bronco. I never knew what to expect. "One day" she continued, "I was friended by my ass." Someone, unbeknownst to her, had made a Facebook profile of Lacey's ass and then friended her. In a subsequent interview, after the class was over, she explained.

> *Lacey:* One day I get on Facebook, and I have a new friend request. I click on it, and I look at it, and it's called "Lacey Gluteus Maximus" as though it is a real name, not Lacey's Gluteus Maximus. And I thought: "that really looks like my butt. That is a picture of my ass." So I friend it, just to find out what is going on, and I get that [question], "How do you know your butt?"[1] So it's like: I'm dating my butt, We hooked up in the year I was born, and it was hot; We're best friends, and...

---

1. When you friend someone, Facebook gives you a menu with preset options to select how you know that person.

Ilana: And what do you choose? I mean, it becomes very complicated.

Lacey: Very complicated. I only did one thing: "I have known my butt since 1987 [when she was born]. And then I get a list back of fifteen things from that person who made the profile. So I go home and I ask my roommate: "Jessie, did you make this?" And she goes: "No, I thought you made it. I got friended by your butt too!" I was like: "What???!? Who did this?" It took me three weeks to find out who did this. It was a friend of mine who is this huge prankster....It cracks me up because Facebook always says "don't put anything inappropriate on Facebook." And people make fake Facebook profiles all the time, and if any are inappropriate, they delete them. I am surprised mine hasn't gotten deleted yet. Maybe they haven't found it because it doesn't have a lot of friends, which is really sad.

This profile of Lacey's ass is not how Facebook designers anticipated Facebook would be used. Lacey kept expecting them to remove the profile, but as I write this, Lacey's ass is still there, available for friending. People keep using Facebook and other new technologies in unexpected ways, as the stories I collected revealed time and time again. While my interviews varied, I could always count on one thing. In each interview, the person I spoke to would mention that they or a friend of theirs used a communicative technology in a way I had not heard of before. We are a long way from standardizing how people use these technologies.

Standardization takes a lot of work. Historians of media have documented the significant amount of conscious education that had to accompany the introduction of telephones, photographs, televisions, and films before "typical" ways of using these technologies were widely established. For example, telephone companies decided it was a problem to have a talkative customer when people had party lines; that is, when several households shared a single telephone line. So, according to historian Claude Fischer in *America's Calling,* "The companies also tried to teach customers to avoid occupying the line with long conversations. They printed notices, had operators intervene, and sent warning letters to particularly talkative customers. In some places, companies imposed time limits that seemed to help, although it is unclear how strictly operators enforced such limits" (Fischer 1992, 71). As Fischer points out, phone companies tried many different tactics as they attempted to educate people on how best to use telephones. When and how people should use telephones instead of in-person conversations was up for grabs. It took a considerable amount of time and effort for the standard ways people nowadays use the telephone to emerge, assisted by companies' and sometimes governments' deliberate pedagogical interventions.

Because of all this effort on the part of companies, schools, and government offices to educate people to use technologies in standard ways, people now expect to have standard practices established. Yet they have not yet developed shared expectations about how to navigate social dilemmas using the new communicative technologies. Asking people about how they use new technologies in the process of breaking up makes this apparent. It is not simply a question of what it means to break up via texting. As I have described, these new technologies raise questions about who should be the first to change their relationship status on Facebook, in what medium is one supposed to respond to the electronically transmitted news of a friend's breakup, when is it appropriate to switch mediums, and so on. As new media allow people more and more options in how they communicate, this variety increases the social dilemmas people face when using these media to connect and, as important, to disconnect with each other. By focusing on breakups, I have been able to highlight the social dilemmas that emerge when shared expectations and etiquette are not yet in place.

Yet because social practices surrounding older media have become standardized, many of the people I interviewed did not realize quite how varied people's practices around new technologies were. Most people thought that there were standard ways to communicate, and they were happy to tell me what these ways were. This can rapidly become a question of ethics. Because I was interviewing people from such different social circles, it was clear to me that people had very different idioms of practice. But the people I interviewed often found themselves dating (sometimes marrying) and then breaking up with people who had very different idioms of practice, yet not always realizing that these differences existed. This is how ethical dilemmas emerge around new technologies: How does one disconnect from someone else ethically when people might have such different understandings of how a particular medium affects messages about disentangling relationships?

I have been laying out some analytical tools people can use to begin to navigate some of the ethical dilemmas that arise. Paying attention to people's media ideologies—to how their beliefs about different media shape how they use these media—can offer insights into the ethics of the situation. And paying attention to media ideologies involves also paying attention to remediation. One cannot understand people's media ideologies for one medium without understanding their media ideologies for other media as well; in short, taking into account people's experiences of remediation. Only by understanding another person's media ideologies in a larger context can you decide if a breakup by text message is so inappropriate that there will be no further communication, or if the message is the technological equivalent of the face-to-face utterance "we have to talk." So much of the interpretive work of ending a relationship can revolve around trying to understand why people are doing what they are doing. Figuring out people's media ideologies, experiences of remediation, and idioms of practice is a first step, although only a first step.

New media spark ethical dilemmas because the media alter the range of information communicated as well as the publics involved. Historians of media have discussed how moral panics will accompany new media because of the ways new forms of disembodied communication transform how people determine each other's social status and trustworthiness. In my interviews, people commented on how a particular medium provides insights into the sender's social context, information which is then used to construct a moral judgment on the sender's practices. In addition, new media allow for the construction of new kinds of publics (Bauman and Feaster 2005). Addressing new publics turns into an ethical question when people are uttering statements that have social and personal consequences such as "I want to break up." New forms of knowledge circulation refigure people's understandings of the ethics surrounding whether information should be public or private, simultaneously also reimagining the boundaries between public and private.

Why does it matter if you break up by text message, by Facebook, or face to face? It matters because people are social analysts of their own lives, because people have developed complex interpretations of how a medium affects a message. For the many people I have spoken to, how people break up is as important to them as the fact that they break up. This makes the media one chooses for breaking up, and the media one chooses in the breakup's aftermath, an ethical choice, and one to be chosen with some care.

Bibliography

Acland, Charles, ed. 2007. *Residual Media*. Minneapolis: University of Minnesota.

Akrich, Madeline. 1992. "The De-scription of a Technical Object." In *Shaping Technology/Building Society: Studies in Sociotechnical Change*, edited by Wiebe E. Bijker, 205–224. Cambridge: The MIT Press.

Anderson, Benedict. 1991. *Imagined Communities*. London: Verso Press.

Barber, Karin. 2007. *The Anthropology of Texts, Persons, and Publics*. Cambridge: Cambridge University Press.

Barker, Joshua. 2008. "Playing with Publics: Technology, Talk, and Sociability in Indonesia." *Language and Society* 28:127–142.

Baron, Naomi. 2008. *Always On: Language in an Online and Mobile World*. Oxford: Oxford University Press.

Bauman, Richard, and Patrick Feaster. 2005. "'Fellow Townsmen and My Noble Constituents!': Representations of Oratory on Early Commercial Recordings." *Oral Tradition* 20:35–57.

Boase, Jeffrey, and Barry Wellman. 2006. "Personal Relationships: On and Off the Internet." In *The Cambridge Handbook of Personal Relationships*, edited by Anita L. Vangelisti and Daniel Perlman, 709–726. Cambridge: Cambridge University Press.

Boellstorff, Tom. 2008. *Coming Of Age in Second Life: An Anthropologist Explores the Virtually Human*. Princeton: Princeton University Press.

Bolter, Jay David, and Richard Grusin. 1999. *Remediation: Understanding New Media*. Cambridge: The MIT Press.

boyd, danah. 2007a. "Viewing American Class Divisions through Facebook and MySpace." *Apophenia Blog Essay*. June 24. http://www.danah.org/papers/essays/ClassDivisions.html.

———. 2007b. "Social Network Sites: Public, Private, or What?" *Knowledge Tree* 13. http://kt.flexiblelearning.net.au/tkt2007/?page_id=28.

———. 2007c. "Why Youth (Heart) Social Network Sites: The Role of Networked Publics in Teenage Social Life." In *Youth, Identity, and Digital Media,* edited by David Buckingham, 119–142. Cambridge: The MIT Press.

———. 2008. "Facebook's Privacy Trainwreck: Exposure, Invasion, and Social Convergence." *Convergence: The International Journal of Research into New Media Technologies* 14(1):13–20. http://con.sagepub.com/cgi/content/abstract/14/1/13.

Caron, André H., and Letizia Caronia. 2007. *Moving Cultures: Mobile Communication in Everyday Life.* Quebec: McGill-Queen's University Press.

Castells, Manuel. 1996. *The Rise of The Network Society.* Malden, MA: Blackwell.

Donath, J., and danah boyd. 2004. "Public Displays of Connection." *BT Technology Journal* 22:71–82.

Ellison, Nicole, Charles Steinfield, and Cliff Lampe. 2007. "The Benefits of Facebook 'Friends': Social Capital and College Students' Use of Online Social Network Sites." *Journal of Computer-Mediated Communication* 12, article 1. http://jcmc.indiana.edu/vol13/issue1/boyd.ellison.html.

Fischer, Claude. 1992. *America Calling: A Social History of the Telephone to 1940.* Berkeley: University of California Press.

Fuller, Matthew. 2005. *Media Ecologies: Materialist Energies in Art and Technoculture.* Cambridge: The MIT Press.

Gal, Susan. 2002. "A Semiotics of the Public/Private Distinction." *differences* 13:77–95.

———. 2005. "Language Ideologies Compared: Metaphors and Circulations of Public and Private." *Journal of Linguistic Anthropology* 15:23–37.

Gal, Susan, and Kathryn Woolard. 2001. *Languages and Publics: The Making of Authority.* Manchester: St. Jerome Publishing.

Gershon, Ilana. 2008. "Email My Heart: Remediation and Romantic Break-Ups." *Anthropology Today* 24:13–15.

Gitelman, Lisa. 1999. *Scripts, Grooves, and Writing Machines: Representing Technology in the Edison Era.* Stanford: Stanford University Press.

———. 2006. *Always Already New: Media, History, and the Data of Culture.* Cambridge: The MIT Press.

Gitelman, Lisa, and Geoffrey B. Pingree, eds. 2003. *New Media, 1740–1915.* Cambridge: The MIT Press.

Goffman, Erving. 1967. *Interaction Ritual: Essays on Face-to-Face Behavior.* Chicago: Anchor Press.

———. 1981. *Forms of Talk.* Philadelphia: University of Pennsylvania Press.

Gould, Emily. 2008. "Exposed" [and online "Readers' Comments"]. *New York Times Sunday Magazine.* May 25. http://www.nytimes.com/2008/05/25/magazine/25internet-t.html.

Graham, Mark, and Shahram Khosavi. 2002. "Reordering Public and Private in Iranian Cyberspace: Identity, Politics, and Mobilization" *Identities* 9:219–246.

Gray, Mary. 2009. "Negotiating Identities/Queering Desires: Coming Out Online and the Remediation of the Coming Out Story." *Journal of Computer Mediated Communication* 14(4): 1162–1189.

Gross, Ralph, Alessandro Acquisti, and H. John Heinz III. 2005. "Information Revelation and Privacy in Online Social Networks." In *Proceedings of the 2005 ACM [Association for Computing Machinery] Workshop on Privacy in the Electronic Society (WPES),* 71–80. New York: ACM.

Hakken, David. 1999. *Cyborgs@Cyberspace?: An Ethnographer Looks to the Future.* New York: Routledge.

———. 2003. *The Knowledge Landscapes of Cyberspace.* New York: Routledge.

Hamilton, Laura, and Elizabeth Armstrong. 2009. "Gendered Sexuality in Young Adulthood: Double Binds and Flawed Options." *Gender and Society* 23(5): 589–616.

Hayles, N. Katherine. 2005. *My Mother Was a Computer: Digital Subjects and Literary Texts.* Chicago: University of Chicago Press.

Heidegger, Martin. 1954. "The Question Concerning Technology." In *Basic Writings,* edited by David Krell, 283–318. New York: Harper Collins.

Helmreich, Stefan. 1998. *Silicon Second Nature: Culturing Artificial Life in a Digital World.* Berkeley: University of California Press.

Hopper, Joseph. "Oppositional Identities and Rhetoric in Divorce." *Qualitative Sociology* 16:133–156.

Horst, Heather, and Daniel Miller. 2006. *The Cell Phone: An Anthropology of Communication.* Oxford: Berg.

Ito, Mizuko, Daisuke Okabe, and Misa Matsuda. 2005. *Personal, Portable, Pedestrian: Mobile Phones in Japanese Life.* Cambridge: The MIT Press.

Jenkins, Henry. 2006. *Convergence Culture: Where Old and New Media Collide.* New York: New York University Press.

Jones, Graham, and Bambi Schieffelin. 2009. "Enquoting Voices, Accomplishing Talk: Uses of *be + like* in Instant Messaging." *Language and Communication* 29:77–113.

Kendall, Lori. 2002. *Hanging Out in the Virtual Pub: Masculinities and Relationships Online.* Berkeley: University of California Press.

———. 2007. "'Shout Into the Wind, and It Shouts Back': Identity and Interactional Tensions on LiveJournal." *First Monday* 12(9). http://firstmonday.org/htbin/cgiwrap/bin/ojs/index.php/fm/article/viewArticle/2004.

Kittler, Frederich. 1997. *Literature, Media, Information Systems: Essays.* Amsterdam: GB Arts International.

———. 1999. *Gramophone, Film, Typewriter.* Stanford: Stanford University Press.

Kroskrity, Paul, ed. 2000. *Regimes of Language: Ideologies, Polities, and Identities.* Santa Fe, NM: School of American Research.

Latour, Bruno. 1988. *The Pasteurization of France.* Translated by Alan Sheridan and John Law. Cambridge: Harvard University Press.

———. 2005. *Re-Assembling the Social: An Introduction to Actor-Network Theory.* Oxford: Oxford University Press.

Lave, Jean, and Etienne Wenger. 1991. *Situated Learning: Legitimate Peripheral Participation.* Cambridge: Cambridge University Press.

Law, John, and John Hassard, eds. 1999. *Actor Network Theory and After.* Oxford: Blackwell Press.

Manovich, Lev. 2002. *The Language of New Media.* Cambridge: The MIT Press.

Marvin, Carolyn. 1988. *When Old Technologies Were New: Thinking about Electric Communication in the Nineteenth Century.* New York: Oxford University Press.

Masten, Jeffrey, Peter Stallybrass, and Nancy J. Vickers, eds. 1997. *Language Machines: Technologies of Literary and Cultural Production.* New York: Routledge.

Miller, Daniel, and Don Slater. 2000. *The Internet: An Ethnographic Approach.* Oxford: Berg.

Moffat, Michael. 1989. *Coming of Age in New Jersey.* New Brunswick: Rutgers University Press.

Nardi, Bonnie A. 2005. "Beyond Bandwidth: Dimensions of Connection in Interpersonal Communication." *Computer-Supported Cooperative Work* 14:91–130.

Nardi, Bonnie, Diane Schiano, and Michelle Gumbrecht. 2004. "Blogging as Social Activity, or, Would You Let 900 Million People Read Your Diary?" *Proceedings of Computer-Supported Cooperative Work 2004.* New York: ACM Press.

Nathan, Rebekah. 2005. *My Freshman Year: What a Professor Learned By Becoming a Student.* Ithaca, NY: Cornell University Press.

Nicol, Bran. 2006. *Stalking.* London: Reaktion Books.

Peters, John Durham. 1999. *Speaking into the Air: A History of the Idea of Communication.* Chicago: University of Chicago Press.

Pollitt, Katha. 2007. *Learning to Drive: and Other Life Stories.* New York: Random House Press.

Reed, Adam. 2005. "'My Blog is Me': Texts and Persons in UK Online Journal Culture (and Anthropology)." *Ethnos* 70:220–242.

Rosen, Laurence, ed. 1995. *Other Intentions: Cultural Contexts and Attribution of Inner States.* Santa Fe, NM: School of American Research Press.

Sabin, Portia. 2007. "On Sentimental Education Among American College Students." *Teachers College Record* 109:1682–1704.

Schieffelin, Bambi, Kathryn A. Woolard, and Paul V. Kroskrity, eds., 1998. *Language Ideologies: Practice and Theory*. New York: Oxford University Press.

Sconce, Jeffrey. 2000. *Haunted Media: Electronic Presence from Telegraphy to Television*. Durham, NC: Duke University Press.

Silverstein, Michael. 1979. "Language Structure and Linguistic Ideology." In *The Elements: A Parasession on Linguistic Units and Levels*, edited by Paul Clyne, William Hanks, and Carol Hofbauer, 193–247. Chicago: Chicago Linguistic Society.

———. 2001. "The Limits of Awareness." In *Linguistic Anthropology: A Reader*, edited by Alessandro Duranti, 382–401. Malden, MA: Blackwell.

Silvio, Teri. 2006. "Informationalized Affect: The Body in Taiwanese Digital Video Puppetry and COSplay." In *Embodied Modernities: Corporeality, Representation, and Chinese Cultures*, edited by Fran Martin and Larissa Heinrich, 195–217. Honolulu: University of Hawai'i Press.

———. 2007. "Remediation and Local Globalizations: How Taiwan's 'Digital Video Knights-Errant Puppetry' Writes the History of the New Media in Chinese." *Cultural Anthropology* 22:285–313.

Simpson, Bob. 1998. *Changing Families: An Ethnographic Approach to Divorce and Separation*. Oxford: Berg.

Stone, Allucquère Rosanne. 1995. *The War of Technology and Desire at the Close of the Mechanical Age*. Cambridge: The MIT Press.

Thorburn, David, and Henry Jenkins, eds. 2003. *Re-thinking Media Change: The Aesthetics of Transition*. Cambridge: The MIT Press.

Turkle, Sherry. 1995. *Life on the Screen: Identity in the Age of the Internet*. New York: Simon and Schuster.

van Dijck, José. 2007. *Mediated Memories in the Digital Age*. Stanford: Stanford University Press.

Vaughn, Dianne. 1986. *Uncoupling: Turning Points in Intimate Relationships*. New York: Oxford University Press.

Warner, Michael. 2002. *Publics and Counterpublics*. New York: Zone Books.

Wenger, Etienne. 1998. *Communities of Practice: Learning, Meaning and Identity*. Cambridge: Cambridge University Press.

Winner, Langdon. 1980. "Do Artifacts Have Politics?" *Daedalus* 109:121–136.

Woolard, Kathryn, and Bambi Schieffelin. 1994. "Language Ideology." *Annual Review of Anthropology* 23:55–82.

Index

Note: Page numbers followed by an *f* refer to figure illustrations. Page numbers followed by an *n* refer to notes.